ART,
CREATIVITY
& BEAUTY
Quotes

A wise man can learn even from a fool

but a fool can learn from no one.

- Aristophanes -

Introduction

This is one of my passions. Putting together the best thoughts from noteworthy humans throughout the ages.

Sorting them into meaningful categories was the greatest challenge of my first such, endeavor, putting together the *Pocketbook of Quotes: From Socrates to Lebowski.*

Socrates? Lebowski? In the same volume. Shocking! Absolutely shocking!

I am also a firm believer that wisdom and insight are to be found everywhere. Philosophy? Of course! Art and literature? Naturally. Pop culture and music? Why not? So, this is eclectic, to be sure. This collection was easier to compile as we are limiting ourselves to these two categories. And is easy reading given the sprinkling of caricature you will find throughout. Sometimes it indicates a large volume from one source. But now always.

I add them to break things up.

The quotes are what you are here for after all.

Art & Creativity

In this chapter of our quotes book dedicated to art and creativity, we delve into the essence of creativity and expression through the words of renowned artists, philosophers, and thinkers. Each quote serves as a doorway into the boundless realm of artistic imagination, offering insights into the power of visual storytelling, the beauty of abstraction, and the transformative nature of artistic exploration. From Pablo Picasso's iconic declaration that "Art washes away from the soul the dust of everyday life" to Vincent van Gogh's poignant reflection that "I am seeking, I am striving, I am in it with all my heart," these quotes encapsulate the multifaceted nature of art as a mirror reflecting the human experience. As you embark on this journey through the chapters of this book, you are invited to ponder the profound impact of art on society, identity, and the human condition itself.

A. Bartlett Giamattaitt
Teachers believe they have a gift for giving. It drives them with the same irrepressible drive that drives others to create a work of art or a market or a building.

Abraham Lincoln
The highest art is always the most religious, and the greatest artist is always a devout person.

Alan Watts
The art of living… is neither careless drifting on the one hand nor fearful drifting on the other. It consists in being sensitive to each moment, in regarding it as utterly new and unique, in having the mind open and wholly receptive.

Agatha Christie
I don't think necessity is the mother of invention. Invention… arises directly from idleness, possibly also from laziness. To save oneself trouble.

Albert Einstein
Creativity is contagious, pass it on.

____

Imagination is more important than knowledge. For knowledge is limited to all we know and understand, while imagination embraces the entire world, and all there ever will be to know and understand.

____

Creativity is intelligence having fun.

____

True art is characterized by an irresistible urge in the creative artist.

____

The most beautiful thing we can experience is the mysterious. It is the source of all true art and science.

____

It is the supreme art of the teacher to awaken joy in creative expression and knowledge.

Agnes Martin
When I think of art I think of beauty. Beauty is the mystery of life. It is not in the eye it is in the mind. In our minds there is awareness of perfection.

1

Agnes Martin
Art is the concrete representation of our most subtle feelings.

Al Capp
Abstract art: a product of the untalented sold by the unprincipled to the utterly bewildered.

Alan Rickman
If only life could be a little more tender and art a little more robust.

Alanis Morissette
I try to keep a low profile in general. Not with my art, but just as a person.

Albert Camus
A guilty conscience needs to confess. A work of art is a confession.

———

Without freedom, no art art lives only on the restraints it imposes on itself, and dies of all others.

———

A man's work is nothing but this slow trek to rediscover, through the detours of art, those two or three great and simple images in whose presence his heart first opened.

———

Truly fertile music, the only kind that will move us, that we shall truly appreciate, will be a music conducive to dream, which banishes all reason and analysis. One must not wish first to understand and then to feel. Art does not tolerate reason.

Albert Ellis
The art of love is largely the art of persistence.

Aldous Huxley
Perhaps it's good for one to suffer. Can an artist do anything if he's happy? Would he ever want to do anything? What is art, after all, but a protest against the horrible inclemency of life?

———

Europe is so well gardened that it resembles a work of art, a scientific theory, a neat metaphysical system. Man has re-created Europe in his own image.

The finest works of art are precious, among other reasons, because they make it possible for us to know, if only imperfectly and for a little while, what it actually feels like to think subtly and feel nobly.

Alexander Calder
To an engineer, good enough means perfect. With an artist, there's no such thing as perfect.

I paint with shapes.

Alexander Pope
So vast is art, so narrow human wit.

———

True ease in writing comes from art, not chance, as those who move easiest have learned to dance.

———

All nature is but art unknown to thee.

———

A work of art that contains theories is like an object on which the price tag has been left.

———

One science only will one genius fit so vast is art, so narrow human wit.

Alfred Adler
The educator must believe in the potential power of his pupil, and he must employ all his art in seeking to bring his pupil to experience this power.

Alfred de Vigny
Art ought never to be considered except in its relations with its ideal beauty.

Alice Walker
Deliver me from writers who say the way they live doesn't matter. I'm not sure a bad person can write a good book. If art doesn't make us better, then what on earth is it for.

Alvar Aalto
Building art is a synthesis of life in materialised form. We should try to bring in under the same hat not a splintered way of thinking, but all in harmony together.

Ambrose Bierce

Painting:
The art of protecting flat surfaces from the weather, and exposing them to the critic.

Photograph:
a picture painted by the sun without instruction in art.

Logic:
The art of thinking and reasoning in strict accordance with the limitations and incapacities of the human misunderstanding.

Eloquence:
The art of orally persuading fools that white is the color that it appears to be. It includes the gift of making any color appear white.

Amy Lowell
Art is the desire of a man to express himself, to record the reactions of his personality to the world he lives in.

Anaïs Nin
If you do not breathe through writing, if you do not cry out in writing, or sing in writing, then don't write, because our culture has no use for it.

———

It is the function of art to renew our perception. What we are familiar with we cease to see. The writer shakes up the familiar scene, and, as if by magic, we see a new meaning in it.

Anatole France
In art as in love, instinct is enough.

———

The whole art of teaching is only the art of awakening the natural curiosity of young minds for the purpose of satisfying it afterwards.

———

What can be more foolish than to think that all this rare fabric of heaven and earth could come by chance, when all the skill of art is not able to make an oyster!

Andre Gide
Art is a collaboration between God and the artist, and the less the artist does the better.

_____

Art begins with resistance - at the point where resistance is overcome. No human masterpiece has ever been created without great labor.

_____

There is no prejudice that the work of art does not finally overcome.

_____

The sole art that suits me is that which, rising from unrest, tends toward serenity.

Andre Malraux
Art is a revolt against fate. All art is a revolt against man's fate.

Andre Maurois
Memory is a great artist. For every man and for every woman it makes the recollection of his or her life a work of art and an unfaithful record.

Andy Warhol
An artist is somebody who produces things that people don't need to have.

_____

I'm afraid that if you look at a thing long enough, it loses all of its meaning.

_____

Being good in business is the most fascinating kind of art. Making money is art and working is art and good business is the best art.

_____

I think having land and not ruining it is the most beautiful art that anybody could ever want to own.

_____

Land really is the best art.

Ani DiFranco
Art is why I get up in the morning but my definition ends there. You know I don't think it's fair that I'm living for something I can't even define.

_____

Art may imitate life, but life imitates TV.

Anish Kapoor
Artists don't make objects. Artists make mythologies.

Ann Landers
All married couples should learn the art of battle as they should learn the art of making love. Good battle is objective and honest - never vicious or cruel. Good battle is healthy and constructive, and brings to a marriage the principles of equal partnership.

Annie Lennox
For me, pointing and clicking my phone is absolutely fine. People say that isn't the art of photography but I don't agree.

Ansel Adams
You don't take a photograph, you make it.

_____

Not everybody trusts paintings but people believe photographs.

_____

There is nothing worse than a sharp image of a fuzzy concept.

_____

Photography is more than a medium for factual communication of ideas. It is a creative art.

_____

There are worlds of experience beyond the world of the aggressive man, beyond history, and beyond science. The moods and qualities of nature and the revelations of great art are equally difficult to define we can grasp them only in the depths of our perceptive spirit.

Anton Chekhov
There is nothing new in art except talent.

Anton Chekhov
The wealthy are always surrounded by hangers-on science and art are as well.

Aristophanes
Let each man exercise the art he knows.

Aristotle
The aim of art is to represent not the outward appearance of things, but their inward significance.

Those who educate children well are more to be honored than they who produce them for these only gave them life, those the art of living well.

Excellence is an art won by training and habituation. We do not act rightly because we have virtue or excellence, but we rather have those because we have acted rightly. We are what we repeatedly do. Excellence, then, is not an act but a habit.

Every art and every inquiry, and similarly every action and choice, is thought to aim at some good and for this reason the good has rightly been declared to be that at which all things aim.

Homer has taught all other poets the art of telling lies skillfully.

It is Homer who has chiefly taught other poets the art of telling lies skillfully.

Arne Jacobsen
If a building becomes architecture, then it is art.

Arthur Balfour
He has only half learned the art of reading who has not added to it the more refined art of skipping and skimming.

Arthur Conan Doyle
To the man who loves art for its own sake, it is frequently in its least important and lowliest manifestations that the keenest pleasure is to be derived.

Arthur Erickson
Rationalism is the enemy of art, though necessary as a basis for architecture.

Arthur Erickson
Vitality is radiated from exceptional art and architecture.

———

The details are the very source of expression in architecture. But we are caught in a vice between art and the bottom line.

Arthur Schopenhauer
Treat a work of art like a prince. Let it speak to you first.

———

Religion is the masterpiece of the art of animal training, for it trains people as to how they shall think.

Auguste Rodin
I choose a block of marble and chop off whatever I don't need.

Augustus Saint-Gaudens
What garlic is to salad, insanity is to art.

Baltasar Gracian
Nature scarcely ever gives us the very best for that we must have recourse to art.

Barbra Streisand
I've been called many names like perfectionist, difficult and obsessive. I think it takes obsession, takes searching for the details for any artist to be good.

Ben Okri
Magic becomes art when it has nothing to hide.

Benjamin Disraeli
A great city, whose image dwells in the memory of man, is the type of some great idea. Rome represents conquest Faith hovers over the towers of Jerusalem and Athens embodies the pre-eminent quality of the antique world, Art.

Benjamin Franklin
The art of acting consists in keeping people from coughing.

Bertrand Russell
Ethics is in origin the art of recommending to others the sacrifices required for cooperation with oneself.

Beverly Sills
Art is the signature of civilizations.

Bill Evans
I think some young people want a deeper experience. Some people just wanna be hit over the head and, you know, if then they [get] hit hard enough maybe they'll feel something. You know? But some people want to get inside of something and discover, maybe, more richness. And I think it will always be the same; they're not going to be the great percentage of the people. A great percentage of the people don't want a challenge. They want something to be done to them -- they don't want to participate. But there'll always be maybe 15% maybe, 15%, that desire something more, and they'll search it out -- and maybe that's where art is, I think.

Billy Idol
Rock isn't art, it's the way ordinary people talk.

Billy Joel
More than art, more than literature, music is universally accessible.

Billy Sunday
There is nothing in the world of art like the songs mother used to sing.

Blaise Pascal
Chance gives rise to thoughts, and chance removes them no art can keep or acquire them.

Boris Pasternak
Literature is the art of discovering something extraordinary about ordinary people, and saying with ordinary words something extraordinary.

Brad Holland
Surrealism: An archaic term. Formerly an art movement. No longer distinguishable from everyday life.

Brad Renfro
I choose films for their artistic value. I don't need a mansion or a Jaguar. When I leave this Earth, I won't take any money with me. All I will leave behind will be my art.

Brian Eno
I had wanted a tape recorder since I was tiny. I thought it was a magic thing. I never got one until just before I went to art school.

Bruno Bettelheim
Raising children is a creative endeavor, an art rather than a science.

Bryant H. McGill
Courtesy is a silver lining around the dark clouds of civilization it is the best part of refinement and in many ways, an art of heroic beauty in the vast gallery of man's cruelty and baseness.

C. S. Lewis
Friendship is unnecessary, like philosophy, like art... It has no survival value rather it is one of those things that give value to survival.

C. S. Lewis
Even in literature and art, no man who bothers about originality will ever be original: whereas if you simply try to tell the truth (without caring twopence how often it has been told before) you will, nine times out of ten, become original without ever having noticed it.

Camille Paglia
The 1990s, after the reign of terror of academic vandalism, will be a decade of restoration: restoration of meaning, value, beauty, pleasure, and emotion to art and restoration of art to its audience.

———

In an era ruled by materialism and unstable geopolitics, art must be restored to the center of public education.

———

Because most of my career in the classroom has been at art schools I am hyper-aware of the often grotesque disconnect between commentary on the arts and the actual practice or production of the arts.

———

One of the main reasons I am so drawn to Hitchcock is that he planned his shots way in advance on story-boards, which he designed like classic paintings (he was an art connoisseur). It's why he found shooting on set boring - because he had already composed the film in his head.

Madonna remains the most visible performer on the planet, as well as one of the wealthiest, but would anyone seriously say that artistic self-development is her primary motivating principle? She is too busy with Kabbalah, fashion merchandising, adoption melodramas, the gym, and ill-starred horseback riding to study art.

_____

It's high time for the art world to admit that the avant-garde is dead. It was killed by my hero, Andy Warhol, who incorporated into his art all the gaudy commercial imagery of capitalism (like Campbell's soup cans) that most artists had stubbornly scorned.

Carl Jung
What did you do as a child that made the hours pass like minutes? Therein lies the key to your earthly pursuits.

Carl Rogers
The very essence of the creative is its novelty, and hence we have no standard by which to judge it.

Carlos Ruiz Zafón
Every book, every volume you see here, has a soul. The soul of the person who wrote it and of those who read it and lived and dreamed with it. Every time a book changes hands, every time someone runs his eyes down its pages, its spirit grows and strengthens.

Carly Fiorina
You have to master not only the art of listening to your head, you must also master listening to your heart and listening to your gut.

Carmen Electra
People are surprised at how down-to-earth I am. I like to stay home on Friday nights and listen to 'The Art of Happiness' by the Dalai Lama.

Carroll O'Connor
Even a true artist does not always produce art.

_____

All in the Family was intellectual it was art.

Casey Stengel
Ability is the art of getting credit for all the home runs somebody else hits.

Catherine Deneuve
Film is a very young art that is still evolving. Soon, we shall reach a balance between content and technology.

Cesare Pavese
The art of living is the art of knowing how to believe lies. The fearful thing about it is that, not knowing what truth may be, we can still recognize lies.

Cesar A. Cruz
Art should comfort the disturbed and disturb the comfortable.

Charles Baudelaire
Evil is committed without effort, naturally, fatally goodness is always the product of some art.

⸺

What is art? Prostitution.

⸺

To say the word Romanticism is to say modern art - that is, intimacy, spirituality, color, aspiration towards the infinite, expressed by every means available to the arts.

⸺

A frenzied passion for art is a canker that devours everything else.

⸺

Evil is done without effort, naturally, it is the working of fate good is always the product of an art.

Charles Bukowski
If something burns your soul with purpose and desire it's your duty to be reduced to ashes by it. Any other form of existence will be yet another dull book in the library of life.

⸺

To do a dull thing with style-now that's what I call art.

Charles de Lint
The beginning of a friendship, the fact that two people out of the thousands around them can meet and connect and become friends, seems like a kind of magic to me. But maintaining a friendship requires work. I don't mean that as a bad thing. Good art requires work as well.

⸺

Life is like art. You have to work hard to keep it simple and still have meaning.

Charles Horton Cooley
An artist cannot fail it is a success to be one.

Charles Morgan
The art of living does not consist in preserving and clinging to a particular mode of happiness, but in allowing happiness to change its form without being disappointed by the change happiness, like a child, must be allowed to grow up.

Charlie Chaplin
I went into the business for the money, and the art grew out of it. If people are disillusioned by that remark, I can't help it. It's the truth.

Charles Mingus
Anyone can make the simple complicated. Creativity is making the complicated simple.

Charlie Parker
Music is your own experience, your own thoughts, your wisdom. If you don't live it, it won't come out of your horn. They teach you there's a boundary line to music. But, man, there's no boundary line to art.

Charlie Sheen
We're going to shoot one Polaroid per show. I'm going to sign this before it even develops because I know that once it develops with my signature on it, it's worth a fortune. I'll make this a work of magic warlock art.

Chinua Achebe
Art is man's constant effort to create for himself a different order of reality from that which is given to him.

Christian Bale
Art is something to be proud of. Art is no compromise.

Christopher Marlowe
O, thou art fairer than the evening air clad in the beauty of a thousand stars.

Clara Schumann
My imagination can picture no fairer happiness than to continue living for art.

Claude Debussy
Art is the most beautiful deception of all. And although people try to incorporate the everyday events of life in it, we must hope that it will remain a deception lest it become a utilitarian thing, sad as a factory.

Claude Monet
Everyone discusses my art and pretends to understand, as if it were necessary to understand, when it is simply necessary to love.

Clive Bell
A rose is the visible result of an infinitude of complicated goings on in the bosom of the earth and in the air above, and similarly a work of art is the product of strange activities in the human mind.

Confucius
It does not matter how slowly you go as long as you do not stop.

———

Imagination is more important than knowledge.

———

Speak the truth, do not yield to anger give, if thou art asked for little by these three steps thou wilt go near the gods.

Conrad Hall
I realize that every picture isn't a work of art.

Cyril Connolly
The artist one day falls through a hole in the brambles, and from that moment he is following the dark rapids of an underground river which may sometimes flow so near to the surface that the laughing picnic parties are heard above.

Deepak Chopra
The best use of imagination is creativity. The worst use of imagination is anxiety.

———

Non-judgment quiets the internal dialogue, and this opens once again the doorway to creativity.

Douglas Adams
Don't you understand that we need to be childish in order to understand? Only a child sees things with perfect clarity, because it hasn't developed all those filters which prevent us from seeing things that we don't expect to see.

Leonardo Da Vinci
The poet ranks far below the painter in the representation of visible things, and far below the musician in that of invisible things.

————

Art is never finished, only abandoned.

————

Where the spirit does not work with the hand, there is no art.

————

The human foot is a masterpiece of engineering and a work of art.

Dale Carnegie
The essence of all art is to have pleasure in giving pleasure.

Damien Hirst
In an artwork you're always looking for artistic decisions, so an ashtray is perfect. An ashtray has got life and death.

Damien Hirst
I always feel like the art's there and I just see it, so it's not really a lot of work.

Danica McKellar
One of the most amazing things about mathematics is the people who do math aren't usually interested in application, because mathematics itself is truly a beautiful art form. It's structures and patterns, and that's what we love, and that's what we get off on.

Danny Boyle
I've sort of escaped my background, as people often do, through art and culture.

Dante Alighieri
Art, as far as it is able, follows nature, as a pupil imitates his master thus your art must be, as it were, God's grandchild.

Dave Barry
It was Public Art, defined as art that is purchased by experts who are not spending their own personal money.

David Bailey
Fashion often starts off beautiful and becomes ugly, whereas art starts off ugly sometimes and becomes beautiful.

David Byrne
It seems almost backwards to me that my music seems the more emotional outlet, and the art stuff seems more about ideas.

David Foster Wallace
The problem is that once the rules of art are debunked, and once the unpleasant realities the irony diagnoses are revealed and diagnosed, 'then' what do we do?

David Herbert Lawrence
The business of art is to reveal the relation between man and his environment.

____

Design in art, is a recognition of the relation between various things, various elements in the creative flux. You can't invent a design. You recognize it, in the fourth dimension. That is, with your blood and your bones, as well as with your eyes.

____

 Oh literature, oh the glorious Art, how it preys upon the marrow in our bones. It scoops the stuffing out of us, and chucks us aside.
Alas!

____

I can't bear art that you can walk round and admire. A book should be either a bandit or a rebel or a man in the crowd.

____

Since obscenity is the truth of our passion today, it is the only stuff of art - or almost the only stuff.

____

The essential function of art is moral. But a passionate, implicit morality, not didactic. A morality which changes the blood, rather than the mind.

David Hockney
The moment you cheat for the sake of beauty, you know you're an artist.

____

Art has to move you and design does not, unless it's a good design for a bus.

What an artist is trying to do for people is bring them closer to something, because of course art is about sharing. You wouldn't be an artist unless you wanted to share an experience, a thought.

_____

Shadows sometimes people don't see shadows. The Chinese of course never paint them in pictures, oriental art never deals with shadow. But I noticed these shadows and I knew it meant it was sunny.

_____

People criticized me for my photography. They said it's not art.

_____

I went to art school actually when I was sixteen years old.

_____

Anyway I feel myself a bit on the edge on the art world, but I don't mind, I'm just pursuing my work in a very excited way. And there isn't really a mainstream anymore, is there?

David Rockefeller

I owe much to mother. She had an expert's understanding, but also approached art emotionally.

_____

I think of art as the highest level of creativity. To me, it is one of the greatest sources of enjoyment.

David Sedaris

After a few months in my parents' basement, I took an apartment near the state university, where I discovered both crystal methamphetamine and conceptual art. Either one of these things are dangerous, but in combination they have the potential to destroy entire civilizations.

Denis Diderot

When science, art, literature, and philosophy are simply the manifestation of personality they are on a level where glorious and dazzling achievements are possible, which can make a man's name live for thousands of years.

Denis Waitley
Winners have the ability to step back from the canvas of their lives like an artist gaining perspective. They make their lives a work of art - an individual masterpiece.

Dieter F. Uchtdorf
The desire to create is one of the deepest yearnings of the human soul.

Dolly Parton
I don't have anything to say about other people's art and their work.

Don Marquis
Procrastination is the art of keeping up with yesterday.

Doris Humphrey
The Dancer believes that his art has something to say which cannot be expressed in words or in any other way than by
dancing.

Dorothea Lange
Photography takes an instant out of time, altering life by holding it still.

Duke Ellington
Art is dangerous. It is one of the attractions: when it ceases to be dangerous you don't want it.

Dwight D. Eisenhower
Leadership is the art of getting someone else to do something you want done because he wants to do it.

_____

Motivation is the art of getting people to do what you want them to do because they want to do it.

Edgar Degas
Painting is very easy when you don't know how, but very difficult when you do.

_____

Painting is easy when you don't know how, but very difficult when you do.

_____

Art is not what you see, but what you make others see.

Elicia Donze
People hate their own art because it looks like they made it. They think if they get better, it will stop looking like they made it. A better person made it. But there's no level of skill beyond which you stop being you. You hate the most valuable thing about your art.

E. M. Forster
To make us feel small in the right way is a function of art men can only make us feel small in the wrong way.

_____

Works of art, in my opinion, are the only objects in the material universe to possess internal order, and that is why, though I don't believe that only art matters, I do believe in Art for Art's sake.

_____

History develops, art stands still.

_____

The sadness of the incomplete, the sadness that is often Life, but should never be Art.

_____

The work of art assumes the existence of the perfect spectator, and is indifferent to the fact that no such person exists.

Earl Wilson
Courage is the art of being the only one who knows you're scared to death.

Eddie Vedder
I think music is the greatest art form that exists, and I think people listen to music for different reasons, and it serves different purposes. Some of it is background music, and some of it is things that might affect a person's day, if not their life, or change an attitude. The best songs are the ones that make you feel something.

Edgar Allan Poe
Were I called on to define, very briefly, the term Art, I should call it 'the reproduction of what the Senses perceive in Nature through the veil of the soul.' The mere imitation, however accurate, of what is in Nature, entitles no man to the sacred name of 'Artist.'

Edgard Varese
An artist is never ahead of his time but most people are far behind theirs.

Edith Wharton
Another unsettling element in modern art is that common symptom of
immaturity, the dread of doing what has been done
before.

―――

Another unsettling element in modern art is that common symptom of
immaturity, the dread of doing what has been done
before.

Edmund Burke
Religion is essentially the art and the theory of the remaking of man. Man
is not a finished creation.

―――

Poetry is the art of substantiating shadows, and of lending existence to
nothing.

Edvard Munch
For as long as I can remember I have suffered from a deep feeling of
anxiety which I have tried to express in my art.

Edward G. Bulwer-Lytton
In life, as in art, the beautiful moves in curves.

Edward Hopper
Great art is the outward expression of an inner life in the artist, and this
inner life will result in his personal vision of the
world.

―――

In general it can be said that a nation's art is greatest when it most
reflects the character of its people.

―――

In its most limited sense, modern, art would seem to concern itself only
with the technical innovations of the period.

―――

The question of the value of nationality in art is perhaps
unsolvable.

The trend in some of the contemporary movements in art, but by no means all, seems to deny this ideal and to me appears to lead to a purely decorative conception of painting.

Edward Koch
The art of creation is older than the art of killing.

———

Deals are my art form. Other people paint beautifully on canvas or write wonderful poetry. I like making deals, preferably big deals. That's how I get my kicks.

Edward Steichen
Every other artist begins with a blank canvas, a piece of paper the photographer begins with the finished product.

———

When that shutter clicks, anything else that can be done afterward is not worth consideration.

———

Photography is a major force in explaining man to man.

Edwin Louis Cole
Reading is an art form, and every man can be an artist.

Elbert Hubbard
Art is not a thing it is a way.

The sculptor produces the beautiful statue by chipping away such parts of the marble block as are not needed - it is a process of elimination.

———

Art is the beautiful way of doing things. Science is the effective way of doing things. Business is the economic way of doing things.

Elia Kazan
The writer, when he is also an artist, is someone who admits what others don't dare reveal.

_____

I was the hero of the young insurgent working class art movement.

Ella Wheeler Wilcox
So many gods, so many creeds, so many paths that wind and wind while just the art of being kind is all the sad world needs.

_____

You may choose your words like a connoisseur, And polish it up with art, But the word that sways, and stirs, and stays, Is the word that comes from the heart.

Ellen Key
The more horrifying this world becomes, the more art becomes abstract.

Elliott Erwitt
To me, photography is an art of observation. It's about finding something interesting in an ordinary place... I've found it has little to do with the things you see and everything to do with the way you see them.

Emile Zola
The artist is nothing without the gift, but the gift is nothing without work.

Emily Carr
I think that one's art is a growth inside one. I do not think one can explain growth. It is silent and subtle. One does not keep digging up a plant to see how it grows.

Emily Dickinson
Where thou art, that is home.

Emma Albani
I had always loved beautiful and artistic things, though before leaving America I had had very little chance of seeing any.

Emir Kusturica
What you have now is a Hollywood that is pure poison. Hollywood was a central place in the history of art in the 20th century: it was human idealism preserved. And then, like any great place, it collapsed, and it collapsed into the most awful machinery in the world.

Emmet Fox
The art of life is to live in the present moment, and to make that moment as perfect as we can by the realization that we are the instruments and expression of God Himself.

Epicurus
The art of living well and the art of dying well are one.

Eric Carle
Simplify, slow down, be kind. And don't forget to have art in your life – music, paintings, theater, dance, and sunsets.

Eric Hoffer
The best part of the art of living is to know how to grow old gracefully.

Erich Fromm
The capacity to be puzzled is the premise of all creation, be it in art or in science.

Ernest Hemingway
Bullfighting is the only art in which the artist is in danger of death and in which the degree of brilliance in the performance is left to the fighter's honor.

Ernst Fischer
In a decaying society, art, if it is truthful, must also reflect decay. And unless it wants to break faith with its social function, art must show the world as changeable. And help to change it.

Erykah Badu
I'm free. I just do what I want, say what I want, say how I feel, and I don't try to hurt nobody. I just try to make sure that I don't compromise my art in any kind of way, and I think people respect that.

Eugene Delacroix
The artist who aims at perfection in everything achieves it in nothing.

Eugene Ionesco
A work of art I above ll an adventure of the mind.

Ezra Croft
People need art in their houses. They don't need Bed Bath and Beyond dentist-office art. They need weird stuff.

Ezra Pound
It ought to be illegal for an artist to marry. If the artist must marry let him find someone more interested in art, or his art, or the artist part of him, than in him. After which let them take tea together three times a week.

F. Scott Fitzgerald
Great art is the contempt of a great man for small art.

Federico Fellini
All art is autobiographical. The pearl is the oyster's autobiography.

Fernando Pessoa
Art gives us the illusion of liberation from the sordid business of being.

Freddie Mercury
You can do whatever you like with my image, my music, remix it, re-release it, whatever… just never make me boring.

Hayao Miyazaki
Humans have both the urge to create and destroy.

Henry Fielding
Now, in reality, the world have paid too great a compliment to critics, and have imagined them men of much greater profundity than they really are.

Howard Aiken
Don't worry about people stealing your ideas. If your ideas are any good, you'll have to ram them down people's throats.

Fran Lebowitz
Very few people possess true artistic ability. It is therefore both unseemly and unproductive to irritate the situation by making an effort. If you have a burning, restless urge to write or paint, simply eat something sweet and the feeling will pass.

Francis Bacon
Fashion is only the attempt to realize art in living forms and social intercourse.

———

The momentous thing in human life is the art of winning the soul to good or evil.

Frederic Chopin
Simplicity is the final achievement. After one has played a vast quantity of notes and more notes, it is simplicity that emerges as the crowning reward of art.

Francis Ford Coppola
I don't think there's any artist of any value who doesn't doubt what they're doing.

Francoise Sagan
Art must take reality by surprise.

Frank Lloyd Wright
Art for art's sake is a philosophy of the well-fed.

———

The mother art is architecture. Without an architecture of our own we have no soul of our own civilization.

———

Simplicity and repose are the qualities that measure the true value of any work of art.

———

Space is the breath of art.

Frank Wedekind
Any fool can have bad luck the art consists in knowing how to exploit it.

Frank Zappa
Art is making something out of nothing and selling it.

Franklin D. Roosevelt
Art is not a treasure in the past or an importation from another land, but part of the present life of all living and creating peoples.

Franz Liszt
Mournful and yet grand is the destiny of the artist.

Franz Marc
Art is nothing but the expression of our dream the more we surrender to it the closer we get to the inner truth of things, our dream-life, the true life that scorns questions and does not see them.

Frida Kahlo

I paint myself because I am so often alone and because I am the subject I know best.

_____

I paint flowers so they will not die.

_____

I don't paint dreams or nightmares, I paint my own reality.

_____

I paint my own reality. The only thing I know is that I paint because I need to, and I paint whatever passes through my head without any other consideration.

Friedrich Nietzsche

The philosopher's product is his life.

_____

Without music, life would be a mistake.

_____

We have art in order not to die of the truth.

_____

The essence of all beautiful art, all great art, is gratitude.

_____

Art is the proper task of life.

_____

Admiration for a quality or an art can be so strong that it deters us from striving to possess it.

_____

Art is not merely an imitation of the reality of nature, but in truth a metaphysical supplement to the reality of nature, placed alongside thereof for its conquest.

_____

For art to exist, for any sort of aesthetic activity to exist, a certain physiological precondition is indispensable: intoxication.

I do not know what the spirit of a philosopher could more wish to be than a good dancer. For the dance is his ideal, also his fine art, finally also the only kind of piety he knows, his 'divine service.'

_____

When art dresses in worn-out material it is most easily recognized as art.

_____

Sleeping is no mean art: for its sake one must stay awake all day.

_____

Art raises its head where creeds relax.

_____

The bad gains respect through imitation, the good loses it especially in art.

Friedrich Schiller
Art is the right hand of Nature. The latter has only given us being, the former has made us men.

_____

Art is the daughter of freedom.

Harriet Ward Beecher
Every artist dips his brush in his own soul, and paints his own nature into his pictures.

Garry Kasparov
I want to serve chess through games, books that are works of art. I would like to bring the game closer to many people all over the world.

George Bernard Shaw
You use a glass mirror to see your face; you use works of art to see your soul.

_____

The reasonable man adapts himself to the world: the unreasonable one persists in trying to adapt the world to himself. Therefore, all progress depends on the unreasonable man.

_____

Imagination is the beginning of creation.

Without art, the crudeness of reality would make the world unbearable.

_____

A fool's brain digests philosophy into folly, science into superstition, and art into pedantry. Hence University education.

_____

She had lost the art of conversation but not, unfortunately, the power of speech.

_____

You use a glass mirror to see your face you use works of art to see your soul.

_____

The art go government is the organization of idolatry.

George Edward Moore
A great artist is always before his time or behind it.

_____

The hours I spend with you I look upon as sort of a perfumed garden, a dim twilight, and a fountain singing to it. You and you alone make me feel that I am alive. Other men it is said have seen angels, but I have seen thee and thou art enough.

George Jean Nathan
Great art is as irrational as great music. It is mad with its own loveliness.

_____

Criticism is the windows and chandeliers of art: it illuminates the enveloping darkness in which art might otherwise rest only vaguely discernible, and perhaps altogether unseen.

_____

To speak of morals in art is to speak of legislature in sex. Art is the sex of the imagination.

_____

Criticism is the art of appraising others at one's own value.

George Santayana
An artist is a dreamer consenting to dream of the actual world.

The effort of art is to keep what is interesting in existence, to recreate it in the eternal.

_____

It is veneer, rouge, aestheticism, art museums, new theaters, etc. that make America impotent. The good things are football, kindness, and jazz bands.

_____

The love of all-inclusiveness is as dangerous in philosophy as in art.

George V. Higgins
Egotism: The art of seeing in yourself what others cannot see.

Georgia O'Keeffe
I found I could say things with color and shapes that I couldn't say any other way... things I had no words for.

Gertrude Stein
A writer should write with his eyes and a painter paint with his ears.

Gilbert K. Chesterton
Art, like morality, consists in drawing the line somewhere.

_____

Lying in bed would be an altogether perfect and supreme experience if only one had a colored pencil long enough to draw on the ceiling.

Gilbert K. Chesterton
Art consists of limitation. The most beautiful part of every picture is the frame.

———

All architecture is great architecture after sunset perhaps architecture is really a nocturnal art, like the art of fireworks.

Glenn Hughes
Listen to your inner-voice: Surround yourself with loving, nurturing people. Fall in love with your art and find yourself. Music is the great communicator.

Groucho Marx
Politics is the art of looking for trouble, finding it everywhere, diagnosing it incorrectly and applying the wrong remedies.

———

Well, Art is Art, isn't it? Still, on the other hand, water is water. And east is east and west is west and if you take cranberries and stew them like applesauce they taste much more like prunes than rhubarb does. Now you tell me what you know.

Artists who seek perfection in everything are those who cannot attain it in anything.
Gustave Flaubert

———

Of all lies, art is the least untrue.

Guy Kawasaki
Patience is the art of concealing your impatience.

Gwendolyn Brooks
Art hurts. Art urges voyages - and it is easier to stay at home.

H. L. Mencken
Democracy is the art and science of running the circus from the monkey cage.

Harold Coffin
Envy is the art of counting the other fellow's blessings instead of your own.

Harry S. Truman
Art is parasitic on life, just as criticism is parasitic on art.

Harvey Fierstein
Art has the power to transform, to illuminate, to educate, inspire and motivate.

Havelock Ellis
Every artist writes his own autobiography.

_____

All the art of living lies in a fine mingling of letting go and holding on.

Hedy Lamarr
A good painting to me has always been like a friend. It keeps me company, comforts and inspires.

Helen Hayes
I cry out for order and find it only in art.

Helen Rowland
Telling lies is a fault in a boy, an art in a lover, an accomplishment in a bachelor, and second-nature in a married man.

Helena Bonham Carter
I'm not dead and I don't have blue hair but some people say there are similarities. It is usually intolerable to watch myself onscreen but this time it's fine. I think it's beautiful and a real work of art.

Hendrik Willem Van Loon
The arts are an even better barometer of what is happening in our world than the stock market or the debates in congress.

Henri Cartier-Bresson
To me, photography is the simultaneous recognition, in a fraction of a second, of the significance of an event.

_____

The creative act lasts but a brief moment, a lightning instant of give-and-take, just long enough for you to level the camera and to trap the fleeting prey in your little box.

31

Henri Matisse
I don't paint things. I only paint the difference between
things.

———

Time extracts various values from a painter's work. When these values
are exhausted the pictures are forgotten, and the more a picture has to
give, the greater it is.
Henri Matisse

———

What I dream of is an art of balance, of purity and serenity devoid of
troubling or depressing subject matter - a soothing, calming influence
on the mind, rather like a good armchair which provides relaxation from
physical fatigue.

Henry A. Kissinger
Art is man's expression of his joy in labor.

———

Diplomacy: the art of restraining power.

Henry Adams
I am an anarchist in politics and an impressionist in art as well as a
symbolist in literature. Not that I understand what these terms mean,
but I take them to be all merely synonyms of
pessimist.

Henry David Thoreau
This world is but a canvas to our imagination.

Henry Hazlitt
The art of economics consists in looking not merely at the immediate
but at the longer effects of any act or policy it consists in tracing the
consequences of that policy not merely for one group but for all
groups.

Henry James
It is art that makes life, makes interest, makes importance... and I know
of no substitute whatever for the force and beauty of its
process.

Henry James
We work in the dark - we do what we can - we give what we have. Our doubt is our passion and our passion is our task. The rest is the madness of art.

Henry Louis Gates
It's important to debunk the myths of Africa being this benighted continent civilized only when white people arrived. In fact, Africans had been creators of culture for thousands of years before. These were very intelligent, subtle and sophisticated people, with organized societies and great art.

Henry Miller
An artist is always alone - if he is an artist. No, what the artist needs is loneliness.

———

The waking mind is the least serviceable in the arts.

———

Art is only a means to life, to the life more abundant. It is not in itself the life more abundant. It merely points the way, something which is overlooked not only by the public, but very often by the artist himself. In becoming an end it defeats itself.

Henry Moore
A sculptor is a person who is interested in the shape of things, a poet in words, a musician by sounds.

Henry Moore
It is a mistake for a sculptor or a painter to speak or write very often about his job. It releases tension needed for his work.

Henry Rollins
Being an artist is dragging your innermost feelings out, giving a piece of yourself, no matter in which art form, in which medium.

Henry Wadsworth Longfellow
The counterfeit and counterpart of Nature is reproduced in art.

Henry Wadsworth Longfellow
For his heart was in his work, and the heart giveth grace unto every art.

———

Resolve and thou art free.

Henry Ward Beecher
Every artist dips his brush in his own soul, and paints his own nature into his pictures.

Henry Ward Beecher
The art of being happy lies in the power of extracting happiness from common things.

———

To array a man's will against his sickness is the supreme art of medicine.

Herbie Hancock
Music happens to be an art form that transcends language.

Herman Hesse
Wisdom is nothing but a preparation of the soul, a capacity, a secret art of thinking, feeling and breathing thoughts of unity at every moment of life.

Herman Melville
Art is the objectification of feeling.

———

To know how to grow old is the master work of wisdom, and one of the most difficult chapters in the great art of living.

———

You're an actor, are you? Well, all that means is: you are irresponsible, irrational, romantic, and incapable of handling an adult emotion or a universal concept without first reducing it to something personal, material, sensational - and probably sexual!
George Herman

Hillary Clinton
The challenge is to practice politics as the art of making what appears to be impossible, possible.

Hippocrates
Wherever the art of medicine is loved, there is also a love of humanity.

____

Life is short, the art long.

Honore de Balzac
If we could but paint with the hand what we see with the eye.

____

Passion is universal humanity. Without it religion, history, romance and art would be useless.

____

The art of motherhood involves much silent, unobtrusive self-denial, an hourly devotion which finds no detail too minute.

____

What is art? Nature concentrated.

____

All humanity is passion without passion, religion, history, novels, art would be ineffectual.

Horace
A picture is a poem without words.

____

It is no great art to say something briefly when, like Tacitus, one has something to say when one has nothing to say, however, and none the less writes a whole book and makes truth into a liar - that I call an achievement.

Hunter S. Thompson
Politics is the art of controlling your environment.

Igor Stravinsky
Lesser artists borrow, great artists steal.

Ingmar Bergman
Film as dream, film as music. No art passes our conscience in the way film does, and goes directly to our feelings, deep down into the dark rooms of our souls.

Isaac Bashevis Singer
Every creator painfully experiences the chasm between his inner vision and its ultimate expression.

Isaac Bashevis Singer
The greatness of art is not to find what is common but what is unique.

Sir Isaac Newton
The breeze at dawn has secrets to tell you. Don't go back to sleep. You must ask for what you really want. Don't go back to sleep.

_____

My powers are ordinary. Only my application brings me success.

_____

No great discovery was ever made without a bold guess.

_____

Errors are not in the art but in the artificers.

_____

Tact is the art of making a point without making an enemy.

Isadora Duncan
Art is not necessary at all. All that is necessary to make this world a better place to live in is to love - to love as Christ loved, as Buddha loved.

_____

It has taken me years of struggle, hard work and research to learn to make one simple gesture, and I know enough about the art of writing to realize that it would take as many years of concentrated effort to write one simple, beautiful sentence.

Jack Kerouac
The only truth is music.

Jack Nicholson
I just like art. I get pure pleasure from it. I have a lot of wonderful paintings, and every time I look at them I see something different.

Jack White
It is a myth that art has to be sold. It is not like stocking a grocery store where people fill a pushcart. Art is a product that has no apparent need. The salesperson builds the need in the mind of the buyer.

Jackson Pollock
I have no fear of making changes, destroying the image, etc., because the painting has a life of its own.

Every good painter paints what he is.

———

My painting does not come from the easel.

James Humes
The art of communication is the language of leadership.

James Taylor
That's the motivation of an artist - to seek attention of some kind.

James Whistler
An artist is not paid for his labor but for his vision.

James Wolcott
Book-jacket design may become a lost art, like album-cover design, without which late-20th-century iconography would have been pauperized.

Jane Campion
I did this Super-8 film at art school called 'Tissues,' this black comedy about a family whose father has been arrested for child molestation. I was absolutely thrilled by every inch of it, and would throw my projector in the back of my car and show it to anybody who would watch it.

There was a big drive when I was at art school to make you aware of the economy of meaning - after all, this was still during the tail end of minimalism. Being responsible for everything you put in your picture, and being able to defend it. Keeping everything clear around you so you know what is operating. To open the wound and keep it clean.

Jawaharial Nehru
The art of a people is a true mirror to their minds.

Jean Anouilh
Things are beautiful if you love them.

___

Life is very nice, but it lacks form. It's the aim of art to give it some.

Jean Cocteau
An original artist is unable to copy. So he has only to copy in order to be original.

___

Art produces ugly things which frequently become more beautiful with time. Fashion, on the other hand, produces beautiful things which always become ugly with time.

___

An artist cannot speak about his art any more than a plant can discuss horticulture.

___

Emotion resulting from a work of art is only of value when it is not obtained by sentimental blackmail.

___

Film will only became an art when its materials are as inexpensive as pencil and paper.

Jean de La Fontaine
By the work one knows the workman.

Jean Rostand
Beauty in art is often nothing but ugliness subdued.

Jean-Michel Basquiat
I don't think about art when I'm working. I try to think about life.

Jef I. Richards
Creative without strategy is called 'art.' Creative with strategy is called 'advertising.'

Jeff Koons
I think about my work every minute of the day.

Jennifer Aniston
Art is so subjective, and people can react however they want.

Jerzy Kosinski
The principles of true art is not to portray, but to evoke.

―――

The principle of art is to pause, not bypass.

Jet Li
Wushu is a move in Chinese, a physical move. An attack. Wushu is like an art.

Jiddu Krishnamurti
When pure feeling is corrupted by intellect, there is mediocrity. That is what most of us are doing.

Jim Henson
At the University of Maryland, my first year I started off planning to major in art because I was interested in theatre design, stage design or television design.

Jim Hodges
When I make art, I think about its ability to connect with others, to bring them into the process.

Jim Morrison
I think in art, but especially in films, people are trying to confirm their own existences.

Jimi Hendrix
My goal is to be one with the music. I just dedicate my whole life to this art.

Jimmy Carter
Like music and art, love of nature is a common language that can transcend political or social boundaries.

Joan Miro
The works must be conceived with fire in the soul but executed with clinical coolness.

Jodie Foster
I think an artist's responsibility is more complex than people realize.

Johann Wolfgang von Goethe
Personality is everything in art and poetry.

———

The mediator of the inexpressible is the work of art.

———

In art the best is good enough.

———

He who possesses art and science has religion he who does not possess them, needs religion.

———

The biggest problem with every art is by the use of appearance to create a loftier reality.

———

It is after all the greatest art to limit and isolate oneself.

John Berger
What makes photography a strange invention is that its primary raw materials are light and time.

John Ciardi
Modern art is what happens when painters stop looking at girls and persuade themselves that they have a better idea.

John Cloooo
Nothing will stop you from being creative so effectively as the fear of making a mistake.

John Donne
Death be not proud, though some have called thee Mighty and dreadful, for thou art not so. For, those, whom thou think'st thou dost overthrow. Die not, poor death, nor yet canst thou kill me.

John F. Kennedy
If art is to nourish the roots of our culture, society must set the artist free to follow his vision wherever it takes him.

John Keats
The excellency of every art is its intensity, capable of making all disagreeable evaporate.

John Kenneth Galbraith
Politics is the art of choosing between the disastrous and the unpalatable.

Politics is not the art of the possible. It consists in choosing between the disastrous and the unpalatable.

John Lasseter
The art challenges the technology, and the technology inspires the art.

John Lennon
If being an egomaniac means I believe in what I do and in my art or music, then in that respect you can call me that... I believe in what I do, and I'll say it.

John Ruskin
Art is not a study of positive reality, it is the seeking for ideal truth.

Fine art is that in which the hand, the head, and the heart of man go together.

All great art is the work of the whole living creature, body and soul, and chiefly of the soul.

Great nations write their autobiographies in three manuscripts - the book of their deeds, the book of their words and the book of their art.

All that we call ideal in Greek or any other art, because to us it is false and visionary, was, to the makers of it, true and existent.

_____

No art can be noble which is incapable of expressing thought, and no art is capable of expressing thought which does not change.

_____

It is in this power of saying everything, and yet saying nothing too plainly, that the perfection of art consists.

_____

The art which we may call generally art of the wayside, as opposed to that which is the business of men's lives, is, in the best sense of the word, Grotesque.

John Tillotson
The art of using deceit and cunning grow continually weaker and less effective to the user.

John Updike
What art offers is space - a certain breathing room for the spirit.

John W. Gardner
Life is the art of drawing without an eraser.

John Wooden
Be true to yourself, help others, make each day your masterpiece, make friendship a fine art, drink deeply from good books - especially the Bible, build a shelter against a rainy day, give thanks for your blessings and pray for guidance every day.

Jonathan Safran Foer
There's no being wrong in seeing something in art, only being disagreed with.

_____

Literature has drawn a funny perimeter that other art forms haven't.

Jonathan Swift
Vision is the art of seeing what is invisible to others.

Jonathan Swift
Good manners is the art of making those people easy with whom we converse. Whoever makes the fewest people uneasy is the best bred in the room.

Joni Mitchell
Back then, I didn't have a big organization around me. I was just a kid with a guitar, traveling around. My responsibility basically was to the art, and I had extra time on my hands. There is no extra time now. There isn't enough time.

Joseph Beuys
Let's talk of a system that transforms all the social organisms into a work of art, in which the entire process of work is included... something in which the principle of production and consumption takes on a form of quality. It's a Gigantic project.

Joseph Campbell
You can get a lot of work done if you stay with it and are excited and it's play instead of work.

Joseph Conrad
History repeats itself, but the special call of an art which has passed away is never reproduced. It is as utterly gone out of the world as the song of a destroyed wild bird.

———

Only in men's imagination does every truth find an effective and undeniable existence. Imagination, not invention, is the supreme master of art as of life.

———

Any work that aspires, however humbly, to the condition of art should carry its justification in every line.

Joseph Gordon-Levitt
Celebrity doesn't have anything to do with art or craft. It's about being rich and thinking that you're better than everybody else.

Karl Kraus
Science is spectral analysis. Art is light synthesis.

Karl Marx
Art is always and everywhere the secret confession, and at the same time the immortal movement of its time.

Karl Wilhelm Friedrich Schlegel
Art and works of art do not make an artist sense and enthusiasm and instinct do.

Kary Mullis
Art is subject to arbitrary fashion.

Katharine Hepburn
I think most of the people involved in any art always secretly wonder whether they are really there because they're good or there because they're lucky.

Keanu Reeves
The whole aspect of cinema and film festivals should be a moment to come together and celebrate art and humanity. It would be a shame if there was such a divide.

Kesha
What I'm doing is art - it's low-brow art but there's a magic in that.

Khalil Gibran
Art is a step from what is obvious and well-known toward what is arcane and concealed.

―――

I wash my hands of those who imagine chattering to be knowledge, silence to be ignorance, and affection to be art.

Kurt Vonnegut
Go into the arts. I'm not kidding. The arts are not a way to make a living. They are a very human way of making life more bearable. Practicing an art, no matter how well or badly, is a way to make your soul grow, for heaven's sake. Sing in the shower. Dance to the radio. Tell stories. Write a poem to a friend, even a lousy poem. Do it as well as you possibly can. You will get an enormous reward. You will have created something.

―――

To practice any art, no matter how well or badly, is a way to make your soul grow.

Lady Gaga
Every bit of me is devoted to love and art. And I aspire to try to be a teacher to my young fans who feel just like I felt when I was younger. I just felt like a freak. I guess what I'm trying to say is I'm trying to liberate them, I want to free them of their fears and make them feel that they can make their own space in the world.

―――

I am a walking piece of art every day, with my dreams and my ambitions forward at all times in an effort to inspire my fans to lead their life in that way.

―――

What I've discovered is that in art, as in music, there's a lot of truth-and then there's a lie. The artist is essentially creating his work to make this lie a truth, but he slides it in amongst all the others. The tiny little lie is the moment I live for, my moment. It's the moment that the audience falls in love.

―――

I was doing these performance art pop music pieces in the city. And they were a bit on the eccentric side I suppose. So people started to call me Gaga after the Queen song 'Radio Gaga.'

Laurence J. Peter
Originality is the fine art of remembering what you hear but forgetting where you heard it.

Laurie Anderson
I've never really had a hobby, unless you count art, which the IRS once told me I had to declare as a hobby since I hadn't made money with it.

Leonard Cohen
Poetry is just the evidence of life. If your life is burning well, poetry is just the ash.

Lenny Bruce
The only honest art form is laughter, comedy. You can't fake it... try to fake three laughs in an hour - ha ha ha ha ha - they'll take you away, man. You can't.

Leo Burnett
If you don't get noticed, you don't have anything. You just have to be noticed, but the art is in getting noticed naturally, without screaming or without tricks.

Leo Tolstoy

Music makes me forget my real situation. It transports me into a state which is not my own. Under the influence of music I really seem to feel what I do not feel, to understand what I do not understand, to have powers which I cannot have.

———

To say that a work of art is good, but incomprehensible to the majority of men, is the same as saying of some kind of food that it is very good but that most people can't eat it.

———

Art is not a handicraft, it is the transmission of feeling the artist has experienced.

———

It is amazing how complete is the delusion that beauty is goodness.

———

Art is not a handicraft, it is the transmission of feeling the artist has experienced.

Lester Bangs
The first mistake of art is to assume that it's serious.

Lin Yutang
Besides the noble art of getting things done, there is the noble art of leaving things undone. The wisdom of life consists in the elimination of non-essentials.

Lionel Trilling
Immature artists imitate. Mature artists steal.

Lord Byron
The great art of life is sensation, to feel that we exist, even in pain.

Lord Chesterfield
In seeking wisdom thou art wise in imagining that thou hast attained it - thou art a fool.

Lou Reed
How can anybody learn anything from an artwork when the piece of art only reflects the vanity of the artist and not reality?

Louis C. K.
To me, art supplies are always okay to buy.

Louis Kahn
Every time a student walks past a really urgent, expressive piece of architecture that belongs to his college, it can help reassure him that he does have that mind, does have that soul.

Louise Brooks
The great art of films does not consist of descriptive movement of face and body but in the movements of thought and soul transmitted in a kind of intense isolation.

Luc de Clapiers
Patience is the art of hoping.

Lucius Annaeus Seneca
All art is but imitation of nature.

_____

To be able to endure odium is the first art to be learned by those who aspire to power.

_____

If thou art a man, admire those who attempt great things, even though they fail.

Ludwig Erhard
A compromise is the art of dividing a cake in such a way that everyone believes he has the biggest piece.

Ludwig Mies van der Rohe
I don't want to be interesting. I want to be good.

Madeleine L'Engle
When the bright angel dominates, out comes a great work of art, a Michelangelo David or a Beethoven symphony.

_____

I like the fact that in ancient Chinese art the great painters always included a deliberate flaw in their work: human creation is never perfect.

Mae West
Love isn't an emotion or an instinct - it's an art.

Malcolm De Chazal
Art is nature speeded up and God slowed down.

Malcolm Forbes
Diversity: the art of thinking independently
together.

Malcolm Muggeridge
Every happening, great and small, is a parable whereby God speaks to
us, and the art of life is to get the message.

Marc Chagall
Great art picks up where nature ends.

Marc Chagall
When I am finishing a picture, I hold some God-made object up to it - a
rock, a flower, the branch of a tree or my hand - as a final test. If the
painting stands up beside a thing man cannot make, the painting is
authentic. If there's a clash between the two, it's bad
art.

_____

In our life there is a single color, as on an artist's palette, which provides
the meaning of life and art. It is the color of love.

Marcel Proust
Only through art can we emerge from ourselves and know what another
person sees.

Marcus Aurelius
The art of living is more like wrestling than
dancing.

_____

When thou art above measure angry, bethink thee how momentary
is man's life.

Margaret Atwood
What matters is how the art makes you feel.

_____

Any novel is hopeful in that it presupposes a reader. It is,
actually, a hopeful act just to write anything, really, because
you're assuming that someone will be around to [read] it.

The genesis of a poem for me is usually a cluster of words. The only good metaphor I can think of is a scientific one: dipping a thread into a supersaturated solution to induce crystal formation.

Margot Fonteyn
Great artists are people who find the way to be themselves in their art. Any sort of pretension induces mediocrity in art and life alike.

Maria Sharapova
I love to collect modern art.

Marilyn Manson
I think art is the only thing that's spiritual in the world. And I refuse to forced to believe in other people's interpretations of God. I don't think anybody should be. No one person can own the copyright to what God means.

———

Growing up going to Christian school and the concept that you're born a sinner and you don't really have a choice to change who you are has been hammered into my head and created the entire reason why I made art and made a band and made records called 'Antichrist Superstar.'

———

I can't satisfy myself with just trying to tie all of my imagination into music, especially when music is not appreciated as an art form as much as it used to be.

———

Art gives me the freedom I don't have when I make music.

Marshall McLuhan
Ads are the cave art of the twentieth century.

Advertising is the greatest art form of the 20th century.

———

Art at its most significant is a Distant Early Warning System that can always be relied on to tell the old culture what is beginning to happen to it.

———

Art is anything you can get away with.
Marshall McLuhan

Martha Beck
Seek art from every time and place, in any form, to connect with those
who really move you.

Martin Luther
Beautiful music is the art of the prophets that can calm the agitations of
the soul it is one of the most magnificent and delightful presents God
has given us.

———

Next to the Word of God, the noble art of music is the greatest treasure
in the world.

———

Music is the art of the prophets and the gift of
God.

Martin Luther King, Jr.
The art of acceptance is the art of making someone who has just done
you a small favor wish that he might have done you a greater
one.

Marvin Hagler
Oh yeah, I mean every fighter has got be dedicated, learn how to
sacrifice, know what the devotion is all about, make sure you're paying
attention and studying your art.

Mary Baker Eddy
I would no more quarrel with a man because of his religion than I would
because of his art.

Mason Cooley
Art begins in imitation and ends in innovation.

———

Lying just for the fun of it is either art or
pathology.

———

If you are going to break a Law of Art, make the crime
interesting.

———

People believe that photographs are true and therefore cannot be art.

Art seduces, but does not exploit.

Maurice Sendak
I think people should be given a test much like driver's tests as to whether they're capable of being parents! It's an art form. I talk a lot. And I think a lot. And I draw a lot. But never in a million years would I have been a parent. That's just work that's too hard.

Max Eastman
It is art that makes life, makes interest, makes importance and I know of no substitute whatever for the force and beauty of its process.

Maya Angelou
You can't use up creativity. The more you use it, the more you have.

Maya Lin
I try to give people a different way of looking at their surroundings. That's art to me.

Maynard James Keenan
The idea is, if I can't heal from my art, then how can you heal?

Megan Fox
People who don't like me talk about it as though I'm trash because I have tattoos. I find that insane because it's 2008, not the 1950s. Tattoos aren't limited to sailors. It's a form of art I find beautiful. I love it.

Michelangelo
The greatest danger for most of us is not that our aim is too high and we miss it, but that it is too low and we reach it.

Michael Palin
I am not a great cook, I am not a great artist, but I love art, and I love food, so I am the perfect traveller.

Michel de Montaigne
My trade and art is to live.

Michel Foucault
What strikes me is the fact that in our society, art has become something which is only related to objects, and not to individuals, or to life.

Madness is the absolute break with the work of art; it forms the constitutive moment of abolition, which dissolves in time the truth of the work of art.

Michelangelo
A man paints with his brains and not with his hands.

The true work of art is but a shadow of the divine perfection.

_____

Trifles make perfection, and perfection is no trifle.

_____

I am a poor man and of little worth, who is laboring in that art that God has given me in order to extend my life as long as possible.

Miguel Angel Ruiz
Every human is an artist. The dream of your life is to make beautiful art.

Miguel de Cervantes
When thou art at Rome, do as they do at Rome.

_____

Miguel de Cervantes
Tell me thy company, and I'll tell thee what thou art.

Mikhail Baryshnikov
I think art education, especially in this country, which government pretty much ignores, is so important for young people.

Morihei Ueshiba
One does not need buildings, money, power, or status to practice the Art of Peace. Heaven is right where you are standing, and that is the place to train.

_____

There are no contests in the Art of Peace. A true warrior is invincible because he or she contests with nothing. Defeat means to defeat the mind of contention that we harbor within.

Morihei Ueshiba
The art of Peace I practice has room for each of the world's eight million gods, and I cooperate with them all. The God of Peace is very great and enjoins all that is divine and enlightened in every land.

Mos Def
Good art provides people with a vocabulary about things they can't articulate.

Napoleon Bonaparte
A picture is worth a thousand words.

———

You must not fight too often with one enemy, or you will teach him all vour art of war.

Nathaniel Hawthorne
Religion and art spring from the same root and are close kin. Economics and art are strangers.

Neil Gaiman
The one thing you have that nobody else has is you. Your voice, your mind, your story, your vision. So write and draw and build and play and dance and live as only you can.

———

The moment that you feel, just possibly, you are walking down the street naked, exposing too much of your heart and your mind, and what exists on the inside, showing too much of yourself...That is the moment, you might be starting to get it right.

Nelson Mandela
I started to make a study of the art of war and revolution and, whilst abroad, underwent a course in military training. If there was to be guerrilla warfare, I wanted to be able to stand and fight with my people and to share the hazards of war with them.

Nick Cave
I'm very happy to hear that my work inspires writers and painters. It's the most beautiful compliment, the greatest reward. Art should always be an exchange.

Nikola Tesla
The mind is sharper and keener in seclusion and uninterrupted solitude. No big laboratory is needed in which to think. Originality thrives in seclusion free of outside influences beating upon us to cripple the creative mind. Be alone, that is the secret of invention; be alone, that is when ideas are born. That is why many of the earthly miracles have had their genesis in humble surroundings.

Nicolas Chamfort
It is commonly supposed that the art of pleasing is a wonderful aid in the pursuit of fortune but the art of being bored is infinitely more successful.

Nicolas Chamfort
The art of the parenthesis is one of the greatest secrets of eloquence in Society.

Nicolaus Copernicus
Although all the good arts serve to draw man's mind away from vices and lead it toward better things, this function can be more fully performed by this art, which also provides extraordinary intellectual pleasure.

Noam Chomsky
Real popular culture is folk art - coalminers' songs and so forth.

Norah Jones
Success and the art of making music are two different things for me.

Novalis
The artist belongs to his work, not the work to the artist.

O. Henry
Love and business and family and religion and art and patriotism are nothing but shadows of words when a man's starving!

Octavia Butler
Sometimes being a friend means mastering the art of timing. There is a time for silence. A time to let go and allow people to hurl themselves into their own destiny. And a time to prepare to pick up the pieces when it's all over.

Octavio Paz
Art is an invention of aesthetics, which in turn is an invention of philosophers... What we call art is a game.

Og Mandino
The person who knows one thing and does it better than anyone else, even if it only be the art of raising lentils, receives the crown he merits. If he raises all his energy to that end, he is a benefactor of mankind and its rewarded as such.

Oliver Wendell Holmes
Life is painting a picture, not doing a sum.

Orson Welles
The enemy of art is the absence of limitations.

_____

I passionately hate the idea of being with it, I think an artist has always to be out of step with his time.

Oscar Wilde
A work of art is the unique result of a unique temperament.

_____

No great artist ever sees things as they really are. If he did, he would cease to be an artist.

_____

Art is the most intense mode of individualism that the world has known.

_____

Life imitates art far more than art imitates Life.

_____

I regard the theatre as the greatest of all art forms, the most immediate way in which a human being can share with another the sense of what it is to be a human being.

_____

It is through art, and through art only, that we can realise our perfection.

_____

All art is quite useless.

The moment you think you understand a great work of art, it's dead for you.

___

It is only an auctioneer who can equally and impartially admire all schools of art.

___

What we have to do, what at any rate it is our duty to do, is to revive the old art of Lying.

___

Beauty is a form of genius - is higher, indeed, than genius, as it needs no explanation. It is of the great facts in the world like sunlight, or springtime, or the reflection in dark water of that silver shell we call the moon.

___

No object is so beautiful that, under certain conditions, it will not look ugly.

Otto Dix
All art is exorcism. I paint dreams and visions too the dreams and visions of my time. Painting is the effort to produce order order in yourself. There is much chaos in me, much chaos in our time.

Ovid
Art lies by its own artifice.

Robert Frost
Poetry begins in delight and ends in wisdom.

P. J. O'Rourke
I realised the bohemian life was not for me. I would look around at my friends, living like starving artists, and wonder, 'Where's the art?' They weren't doing anything. And there was so much interesting stuff to do, so much fun to be had... maybe I could even quit renting.

Pablo Picasso
The meaning of life is to find your gift. The purpose of life is to give it away.

Bad artists copy. Good artists steal.

———

Every child is an artist, the problem is staying an artist when you grow up.

———

Learn the rules like a pro, so you can break them like an artist.

———

Art is the elimination of the unnecessary.

———

Every act of creation is first an act of destruction.

———

I begin with an idea and then it becomes something else.

———

The hidden harmony is better than the obvious.

———

The chief enemy of creativity is 'good' sense.

———

Art is a lie that makes us realize the truth.

———

The purpose of art is washing the dust of daily life of our souls.

———

The artist is a receptacle for emotions that come from all over the place: from the sky, from the earth, from a scrap of paper, from a passing shape, from a spider's web.

———

Some painters transform the sun into a yellow spot, others transform a yellow spot into the sun.

———

Painting is just another way of keeping a diary.

———

Art is the elimination of the unnecessary.

———

Art is not the application of a canon of beauty but what the instinct and the brain can conceive beyond any canon. When we love a woman we don't start measuring her limbs.

One must act in painting as in life, directly.

———

There is no abstract art. You must always start with something. Afterward you can remove all traces of reality.

———

We all know that Art is not truth. Art is a lie that makes us realize the truth, at least the truth that is given to us to understand.

———

The people who make art their business are mostly imposters.

———

Sculpture is the art of the intelligence.

Paracelsus
Medicine is not only a science it is also an art. It does not consist of compounding pills and plasters it deals with the very processes of life, which must be understood before they may be guided.

———

The art of healing comes from nature, not from the physician. Therefore the physician must start from nature, with an open mind.

Patti Smith
In art and dream may you proceed with abandon. In life may you proceed with balance and stealth.

Paul Cezanne
When I judge art, I take my painting and put it next to a God made object like a tree or flower. If it clashes, it is not art.

———

A work of art which did not begin in emotion is not art

The most seductive thing about art is the personality of the artist himself.

_____

An art which isn't based on feeling isn't an art at all.

_____

Art is a harmony parallel with nature.

_____

My age and health will never allow me to realize the dream of art I've been pursuing all my life.

_____

Don't be an art critic. Paint. There lies salvation.

_____

I am more a friend of art than a producer of painting.

_____

You say a new era in art is preparing you sensed it coming continue your studies without weakening. God will do the rest.

_____

I have nothing to hide in art. The initial force alone can bring anyone to the end he must attain.

_____

Is art really the priesthood that demands the pure in heart who belong to it wholly?

Paul Gauguin
Art is either plagiarism or revolution.

_____

The history of modern art is also the history of the progressive loss of art's audience. Art has increasingly become the concern of the artist and the bafflement of the public.

Paul Getty

The beauty one can find in art is one of the pitifully few real and lasting products of human endeavor.

———

My love of fine art increased - the more of it I saw, the more of it I wanted to see.

Paul Hawken

Good management is the art of making problems so interesting and their solutions so constructive that everyone wants to get to work and deal with them.

Paul Klee

Art does not reproduce what we seee rather, it makes us see.

———

The worst state of affairs is when science begins to concern itself with art.

Paul Rand

Design is the method of putting form and content together. Design, just as art, has multiple definitions there is no single definition. Design can be art. Design can be aesthetics. Design is so simple, that's why it is so complicated.

Paul Strand

The artist's world is limitless. It can be found anywhere, far from where he lives or a few feet away. It is always on his doorstep.

Paul Valery

An artist never really finishes work, he merely abandons it.

Paulo Coelho

We want to answer this classical question, who am I? So I think that most of our works are for art, or whatever we do, including science or religion, tried to answer that question.

Peter De Vries

Murals in restaurants are on par with food in museums.

Philip Johnson
Architecture is the art of how to waste space.

Philip Pullman
There are some themes, some subjects, too large for adult fiction; they can only be dealt with adequately in a children's book.

Pierre Bonnard
A painting that is well composed is half finished.

Pink
I want art to make me think. In order to do that, it may piss me off, or make me uncomfortable. That promotes awareness and change, or at least some discussion.

Plato
The beginning is the most important part of the work.

_____

Rhetoric is the art of ruling the minds of men.

Publilius Syrus
Art has a double face, of expression and illusion, just like science has a double face: the reality of error and the phantom of truth.

Quentin Tarantino
I like it when somebody tells me a story, and I actually really feel that that's becoming like a lost art in American cinema.

Quintilian
The perfection of art is to conceal art.

R. Buckminster Fuller
Parents are usually more careful to bestow knowledge on their children rather than virtue, the art of speaking well rather than doing well but their manners should be of the greatest concern.

Rabindranath Tagore
What is Art? It is the response of man's creative soul to the call of the Real.

_____

In Art, man reveals himself and not his objects.

Rainer Maria Rilke

Surely all art is the result of one's having been in danger, of having gone through an experience all the way to the end, where no one can go any further.

———

No great art has ever been made without the artist having known danger.

Ralph Waldo Emerson

Every artist was first an amateur.

———

In art, the hand can never execute anything higher than the heart can imagine.

———

Pictures must not be too picturesque.

———

Love of beauty is taste. The creation of beauty is art.

Ray Bradbury

Science fiction is any idea that occurs in the head and doesn't exist yet, but soon will, and will change everything for everybody, and nothing will ever be the same again. As soon as you have an idea that changes some small part of the world you are writing science fiction. It is always the art of the possible, never the impossible.

Raymond Chandler

Everything a writer learns about the art or craft of fiction takes just a little away from his need or desire to write at all. In the end he knows all the tricks and has nothing to say.

Rebecca West

Any authentic work of art must start an argument between the artist and his audience.

Kate Reid

Acting is not being emotional, but being able to express emotion.

Remy de Gourmont
Aesthetic emotion puts man in a state favorable to the reception of erotic emotion. Art is the accomplice of love. Take love away and there is no longer art.

Rene Magritte
Art evokes the mystery without which the world would not exist.

Richard Roeper
Men's magazines often feature pictures of naked ladies. Women's magazines also often feature pictures of naked ladies. This is because the female body is a beautiful work of art, while the male body is hairy and lumpy and should not be seen by the light of day.

Rick Springfield
I think good art does come from a dark place.

Rita Mae Brown
Art is moral passion married to entertainment. Moral passion without entertainment is propaganda, and entertainment without moral passion is television.

Robert Browning
It is the glory and good of Art, That Art remains the one way possible Of speaking truth, to mouths like mine at least.

_____

Thou art my single day, God lends to leaven What were all earth else, with a feel of heaven.

ᘒ   ᘓ

Robert Carlyle
My first love is art, and I see a lot of things in an artistic way.

Robert Delaunay
Vision is the true creative rhythm.

Painting is by nature a luminous language.

_____

Light in Nature creates the movement of colors.

_____

Art in Nature is rhythmic and has a horror of constraint.

Robert Frost
Take care to sell your horse before he dies. The art of life is passing losses on.

Robert Hughes
The new job of art is to sit on the wall and get more expensive.

Robert Indiana
I think of my peace paintings as one long poem, with each painting being a single stanza.

———

I was the least Pop of all the Pop artists.

———

I realize that protest paintings are not exactly in vogue, but I've done many.

ॐ   ॐ

Robert Louis Stevenson
The web, then, or the pattern, a web at once sensuous and logical, an elegant and pregnant texture: that is style, that is the foundation of the art of literature.

Robert Mapplethorpe
When I work, and in my art, I hold hands with God.

———

To make pictures big is to make them more powerful.

ॐ   ॐ

Robert Morgan
Alchemy is the art of far and near, and I think poetry is alchemy in that way. It's delightful to distort size, to see something that's tiny as though it were vast.

———

The idea of avant-garde art is a very suspicious thing to me, the idea that poetry is new and it keeps being new the way Chevrolets every year are new.

ॐ   ॐ

Robert Motherwell
Wherever art appears, life disappears.

Robert Rauschenberg
You begin with the possibilities of the material.

Robert Schumann
To send light into the darkness of men's hearts - such is the duty of the artist.

Robert Smithson
Artists themselves are not confined, but their output is.

Roy Lichtenstein
I like to pretend that my art has nothing to do with me.

———

Roy Lichtenstein
Art doesn't transform. It just plain forms.

Rudyard Kipling
And the first rude sketch that the world had seen was joy to his mighty heart, till the Devil whispered behind the leaves 'It's pretty, but is it Art?'

———

It's clever, but is it Art?

John Ruskin
He is the greatest artist who has embodied, in the sum of his works, the greatest number of the greatest ideas.

Russell Simmons
Art allows people a way to dream their way out of their struggle.

Saint Augustine
Thou must be emptied of that wherewith thou art full, that thou mayest be filled with that whereof thou art empty.

Salma Hayek
I have a small house so I borrow everything except art, that's what I love.

Salvador Dali

Those who do not want to imitate anything, produce nothing.

———

Drawing is the honesty of the art. There is no possibility of cheating. It is either good or bad.

———

Painting is an infinitely minute part of my personality.

———

Drawing is the honesty of the art. There is no possibility of cheating. It is either good or bad.

———

Painting is an infinitely minute part of my personality.

———

The terrifying and edible beauty of Nouveau architecture.

———

Progressive art can assist people to learn not only about the objective forces at work in the society in which they live, but also about the intensely social character of their interior lives. Ultimately, it can propel people toward social emancipation.

———

We are all hungry and thirsty for concrete images. Abstract art will have been good for one thing: to restore its exact virginity to figurative art.

Samuel Butler

The history of art is the history of revivals.

———

Life is not an exact science, it is an art.

———

Life is the art of drawing sufficient conclusions from insufficient premises.

The sinews of art and literature, like those of war, are money.

–––

The youth of an art is, like the youth of anything else, its most interesting period. When it has come to the knowledge of good and evil it is stronger, but we care less about it.

Samuel Johnson
Poetry is the art of uniting pleasure with truth.

–––

The true art of memory is the art of attention.

–––

There is nothing, Sir, too little for so little a creature as man. It is by studying little things that we attain the great art of having as little misery and as much happiness as possible.

Sarah Bernhardt
What matters poverty? What matters anything to him who is enamoured of our art? Does he not carry in himself every joy and every beauty?

Sarah McLachlan
Trying to force creativity is never good.

Saul Bellow
What is art but a way of seeing?

Saul Williams
The downfall of the industry seems to actually be good for art. I think the industry will find their way once the focus shifts from its greed-based origins, downsizes, and begins to support creative visions that speak to our times and shifting ideals.

Johann Von Schiller
Art is the right hand of Nature. The latter has only given us being, the former has made us men.

Scott Adams
Creativity is allowing yourself to make mistakes. Art is knowing which ones to keep.

Sean Thompson
Creativity is its own reward. If allowed, it feeds itself,
so never let it go hungry.

———

Free access to human creativity is a birthright.

———

Creativity is its own reward. If allowed, it feeds itself,
so never let it go hungry.

Sherman Alexie
All I owe the world is my art.

Shirley MacLaine
I'd like to introduce someone who has just come into my life. I've
admired him for 35 years. He's someone who represents integrity,
honesty, art, and on top of that stuff I'm actually sleeping with
him.

Simone de Beauvoir
To catch a husband is an art to hold him is a job.

———

Art is an attempt to integrate evil.

Simone Weil
To want friendship is a great fault. Friendship ought to be a gratuitous
joy, like the joys afforded by art or life.

Simone Weil
Most works of art, like most wines, ought to be consumed in the
district of their fabrication.

Simonides
Painting is silent poetry, and poetry is painting that speaks.

Socrates
Be slow to fall into friendship but when thou art in,
continue firm and constant.

Sri Chinmoy
If we know the divine art of concentration, if we know the divine art of meditation, if we know the divine art of contemplation, easily and consciously we can unite the inner world and the outer world.

Stanislaw Lec
Youth is the gift of nature, but age is a work of art.

Stanley Kubrick
The screen is a magic medium. It has such power that it can retain interest as it conveys emotions and moods that no other art form can hope to tackle.

Stella Adler
Life beats down and crushes the soul and art reminds you that you have one.

Stendhal
The man of genius is he and he alone who finds such joy in his art that he will work at it come hell or high water.

———

Logic is neither an art nor a science but a dodge.

Art, in itself, is an attempt to bring order out of chaos.
Stephen Sondheim

Steve Jobs
If you are working on something exciting that you really care about you don't have to be pushed. The vision pulls you.

———

Creativity is just connecting things. When you ask creative people how they did something, they feel a little guilty because they didn't really do it, they just saw something. It seemed obvious to them after a while.

Steve Martin
I believe entertainment can aspire to be art, and can become art, but if you set out to make art you're an idiot.

There's a lot of thought in art. People get to talk about important things. There's a lot of sex, you know, in art. There's a lot of naked women and men, and there's intrigue, there's fakery. It's a real microcosm of the larger world.

———

You want to be a bit compulsive in your art or craft or whatever you do.

———

I'm enamored with the art world. Anytime you look at anything that's considered artistic, there's a commercial world around it: the ballet, opera, any kind of music. It can't exist without it.

Steve Prefontaine
A race is a work of art that people can look at and be affected in as many ways they're capable of understanding.

Steven Spielberg
I don't think any movie or any book or any work of art can solve the stalemate in the Middle East today. But it's certainly worth a try.

Sun Tzu
The supreme art of war is to subdue the enemy without fighting.

———

In the practical art of war, the best thing of all is to take the enemy's country whole and intact to shatter and destroy it is not so good.

Susan Cain
The secret to life is to put your self in the right lighting. For some, it's a Broadway spotlight; for others, a lamplit desk. Use your natural powers - of persistence, concentration, and insight - to do work you love and work that matters. Solve problems. Make art. Think deeply.

Interpretation is the revenge of the intellectual upon art.

Susan Sontag
Interpretation is the revenge of the intellectual upon art.

Sydney Pollack
I didn't grow up thinking of movies as film, or art, but as movies, something to do on a Saturday afternoon.

Sylvia Plath
Dying is an art, like everything else. I do it exceptionally well. I do it so it feels like hell. I do it so it feels real. I guess you could say I've a call.

T. S. Eliot
Art never improves, but... the material of art is never quite the same.

Tadao Ando
My hand is the extension of the thinking process - the creative process.

Temple Grandin
Mild autism can give you a genius like Einstein. If you have severe autism, you could remain nonverbal. You don't want people to be on the severe end of the spectrum. But if you got rid of all the autism genetics, you wouldn't have science or art. All you would have is a bunch of social 'yak yaks.'

Tennessee Williams
All good art is an indiscretion.

Theodor Adorno
Art is magic delivered from the lie of being truth.

The task of art today is to bring chaos into order.

Every work of art is an uncommitted crime.

Art is permitted to survive only if it renounces the right to be different, and integrates itself into the omnipotent realm of the profane.

Theodor Adorno
Everything that has ever been called folk art has always reflected domination.

Theodore Bikel
No heirloom of humankind captures the past as do art and language.

In my world, history comes down to language and art. No one cares much about what battles were fought, who won them and who lost them - unless there is a painting, a play, a song or a poem that speaks of the event.

Theodore Dreiser
Art is the stored honey of the human soul, gathered on wings of misery and travail.

Thom Yorke
One of the interesting things here is that the people who should be shaping the future are politicians. But the political framework itself is so dead and closed that people look to other sources, like artists, because art and music allow people a certain freedom.

_____

I think no artist can claim to have any access to the truth, or an authentic version of an event. But obviously they have slightly better means at their disposal because they have their art to energize whatever it is they're trying to write about. They have music.

Thomas A. Edison
To my mind the old masters are not art their value is in their scarcity.

Thomas Aquinas
The knowledge of God is the cause of things. For the knowledge of God is to all creatures what the knowledge of the artificer is to things made by his art.

Thomas Browne
All things are artificial, for the nature is the art of God.

_____

Every man should follow the bent of his nature in art and letters, always provided that he does not offend against the rules of morality and good taste.

Thomas Hardy
Poetry is emotion put into measure. The emotion must come by nature, but the measure can be acquired by art.

_____

Thomas Huxley
In science, as in art, and, as I believe, in every other sphere of human activity, there may be wisdom in a multitude of counsellors, but it is only in one or two of them.

Thomas Kincade
I view art as an inspirational tool.

Thomas Mann
An art whose medium is language will always show a high degree of critical creativeness, for speech is itself a critique of life: it names, it characterizes, it passes judgment, in that it creates.

Thomas Merton
Art enables us to find ourselves and lose ourselves at the same time.

Thomas Wolfe
Culture is the arts elevated to a set of beliefs.

Tom Stoppard
Skill without imagination is craftsmanship and gives us many useful objects such as wickerwork picnic baskets. Imagination without skill gives us modern art.

It is not hard to understand modern art. If it hangs on a wall it's a painting, and if you can walk around it it's a sculpture.

———

You can't but know that if you can capture the emotions of the audience as well as their minds, the play will work better, because it's a narrative art form.

Tony Blair
The art of leadership is saying no, not saying yes. It is very easy to say yes.

Tony Hawk
I consider skateboarding an art form, a lifestyle and a sport. 'Action sport' would be the least offensive categorization.

Tony Snow
The art of being sick is not the same as the art of getting well.

Trudy Jane
Some people will always be deaf to your song. Don't stop signing.

T.S. Eliot
The purpose of literature is to turn blood into ink.

Twyla Tharp
Art is the only way to run away without leaving home.

Ulysses S. Grant
The art of war is simple enough. Find out where your enemy is. Get at him as soon as you can. Strike him as hard as you can, and keep moving on.

Umberto Eco
Translation is the art of failure.

Unknown
What garlic is to food, insanity is to art.

Unknown
A critic is a legless man who teaches running.

Ursula K. Le Guin
The creative adult is the child who survived.

Valentino Rossi
Riding a race bike is an art - a thing that you do because you feel something inside.

Victor Hugo
Dear God! how beauty varies in nature and art. In a woman the flesh must be like marble in a statue the marble must be like flesh.

I am a soul. I know well that what I shall render up to the grave is not myself. That which is myself will go elsewhere. Earth, thou art not my abyss!

Freedom in art, freedom in society, this is the double goal towards which all consistent and logical minds must strive.

Vidal Sassoon
For nine years I worked to change what was hairdressing then into a geometric art form with color, perm without setting which had never been done before.

Vincent van Gogh
If you hear a voice within you say 'you cannot paint,' then by all means paint, and that voice will be silenced.

Art is to console those who are broken by life.

_____

A grain of madness is the best of art.

Virginia Woolf
Really I don't like human nature unless all candied over with art.

Vladimir Nabokov
A work of art has no importance whatever to society. It is only important to the individual.

Voltaire
Originality is nothing but judicious imitation.

_____

The secret to being boring is to say everything.

_____

In general, the art of government consists of taking as much money as possible from one class of citizens to give to another.

_____

The art of government is to make two-thirds of a nation pay all it possibly can pay for the benefit of the other third.

_____

The art of medicine consists in amusing the patient while nature cures the disease.

W. H. Auden
'Healing,' Papa would tell me, 'is not a science, but the intuitive art of wooing nature.'

W. H. Auden
It is a sad fact about our culture that a poet can earn much more money writing or talking about his art than he can by practicing it.

W. Somerset Maugham
Every production of an artist should be the expression of an adventure of his soul.

Walt Disney
I never called my work an 'art'. It's part of show business, the business of building entertainment.

Walt Whitman
The art of art, the glory of expression and the sunshine of the light of letters, is simplicity.

———

I say that democracy can never prove itself beyond cavil, until it founds and luxuriantly grows its own forms of art, poems, schools, theology, displacing all that exists, or that has been produced anywhere in the past, under opposite influences.

Walter Benjamin
The greater the decrease in the social significance of an art form, the sharper the distinction between criticism and enjoyment by the public. The conventional is uncritically enjoyed, and the truly new is criticized with aversion.

———

The art of storytelling is reaching its end because the epic side of truth, wisdom, is dying out.

Walter Hagen
It is the addition of strangeness to beauty that constitutes the romantic character in art.

Walter Murch
Film editing is now something almost everyone can do at a simple level and enjoy it, but to take it to a higher level requires the same dedication and persistence that any art form does.

Walter Winchell
Gossip is the art of saying nothing in a way that leaves practically nothing unsaid.

Will Durant
Every science begins as philosophy and ends as art.

———

To say nothing, especially when speaking, is half the art of diplomacy.

Will Rogers
Diplomacy is the art of saying 'Nice doggie' until you can find a rock.

———

Advertising is the art of convincing people to spend money they don't have for something they don't need.

Will Smith
When you create art, the world has to wait.

William Bernbach
Advertising is fundamentally persuasion and persuasion happens to be not a science, but an art.

William Blake
What is Poetry? To see a world in a grain of sand and heaven in a wild flower. Hold infinity in the palm of your hand and eternity in a hour.

———

He who would do good to another must do it in Minute Particulars: general Good is the plea of the scoundrel, hypocrite, and flatterer, for Art and Science cannot exist but in minutely organized Particulars.

———

Art can never exist without naked beauty displayed.

———

Art is the tree of life. Science is the tree of death.

———

The foundation of empire is art and science. Remove them or degrade them, and the empire is no more. Empire follows art and not vice versa as Englishmen suppose.

William Faulkner
The aim of every artist is to arrest motion, which is life, by artificial means and hold it fixed so that a hundred years later, when a stranger looks at it, it moves again since it is life.

William Hazlitt
Rules and models destroy genius and art.

———

The art of life is to know how to enjoy a little and to endure very much.

———

Cunning is the art of concealing our own defects, and discovering other people's weaknesses.

———

Life is the art of being well deceived and in order that the deception may succeed it must be habitual and uninterrupted.

———

The art of pleasing consists in being pleased.

William James
The art of being wise is the art of knowing what to overlook.

William Morris
I do not want art for a few any more than education for a few, or freedom for a few.

———

So long as the system of competition in the production and exchange of the means of life goes on, the degradation of the arts will go on and if that system is to last for ever, then art is doomed, and will surely die that is to say, civilization will die.

———

If you cannot learn to love real art at least learn to hate sham art.

William Ralph Inge
Literature flourishes best when it is half a trade and half an art.

William Shakespeare
There's no art to find the mind's construction in the face.

William Wordsworth
Pictures deface walls more often than they decorate them.

Wilson Mizner
Art is science made clear.

———

It is not in life, but in art that self-fulfillment is to be found.

Winston Churchill
Without tradition, art is a flock of sheep without a shepherd. Without innovation, it is a corpse.

Wole Soyinka
But theater, because of its nature, both text, images, multimedia effects, has a wider base of communication with an audience. That's why I call it the most social of the various art forms.

Woody Allen
Life doesn't imitate art, it imitates bad television.

Yoko Ono
Controversy is part of the nature of art and creativity.

 Beauty

And now for the corollary of art, beauty. In this chapter of our quotes book dedicated to beauty, we embark on a journey through the myriad expressions of allure, grace, and aesthetic wonder. From the timeless wisdom of Ralph Waldo Emerson, who declared, "Never lose an opportunity of seeing anything beautiful, for beauty is God's handwriting," to the modern-day musings of unknown authors reminding us that "Next time you think of beautiful things, don't forget to count yourself in," each quote encapsulates the essence of beauty in its purest form. Prepare to be captivated by the elegance of language as we explore the profound connections between inner radiance and external magnificence. Whether you seek inspiration, solace, or simply a moment of appreciation for the world's splendor, let these quotes be your guiding light through the tapestry of beauty.

Adam Carolla
The very definition of 'beauty' is outside.

Adam Schiff
Unless action is taken soon - unless we can display the same vision of that earlier period - we will lose the treasure of California's open space and environmental beauty.

Albert Einstein
A human being experiences himself, his thoughts and feelings as something separated from the rest, a kind of optical delusion of consciousness. This delusion is a kind of prison for us, restricting us to our personal desires and to affection for a few persons nearest to us. Our task must be to free ourselves from this prison by widening our circle of compassion to embrace all living creatures and the whole of nature in its beauty.

Adlai E. Stevenson
A beauty is a woman you notice a charmer is one who notices you.

Agnes Martin
When I think of art I think of beauty. Beauty is the mystery of life. It is not in the eye it is in the mind. In our minds there is awareness of perfection.

Akhenaton
When virtue and modesty enlighten her charms, the lustre of a beautiful woman is brighter than the stars of heaven, and the influence of her power it is in vain to resist.

Alanis Morissette
In LA, where I live, it's all about perfectionism. Beauty is now defined by your bones sticking out of your decolletage. For that to be the standard is really perilous for women.

―――

Beauty is now defined by your bones sticking out of your decolletage. For that to be the standard is really perilous for women.

Albert Camus
Beauty is unbearable, drives us to despair, offering us for a minute the glimpse of an eternity that we should like to stretch out over the whole of time.

―――

Beauty is unbearable, drives us to despair, offering us for a minute the glimpse of an eternity that we should like to stretch out over the whole of time.

Albert Einstein
The pursuit of truth and beauty is a sphere of activity in which we are permitted to remain children all our lives.

Alberto Korda
The beauty of women was the first expression of my photography.

Albrecht Durer
No single man can be taken as a model for a perfect figure, for no man lives on earth who is endowed with the whole of beauty.

Aldous Huxley
Beauty is worse than wine, it intoxicates both the holder and beholder.

Alessandra Ambrosio
One of my favorite beauty products is Vincent Longo Water Canvas creamy blush. I have it in every color and I've been using it for 5 years and that's all I put on when I leave the house. It looks so natural I just put a little bit on my cheeks to give them some color.

Alexander Alekhine
I believe that true beauty of chess is more than enough to satisfy all possible demands.

———

Oh! this opponent, this collaborator against your will, whose notion of beauty always differs from yours and whose means are often too limited for active assistance to your intentions!

Alexander Herzen
What breadth, what beauty and power of human nature and development there must be in a woman to get over all the palisades, all the fences, within which she is held captive!

Alexander McQueen
I find beauty in the grotesque, like most artists.

Alexis Arguello
When you put the interest of a kid on money instead of heart then you're destroying the beauty of our lives and our thought process, which should be about how much responsibilities you carry as an athlete and a citizen.

Alfred Jarry
It is conventional to call 'monster' any blending of dissonant elements. I call 'monster' every original inexhaustible beauty.

Alicia Machado
Beauty is only temporary, but your mind lasts you a lifetime.

Allison Janney
I'd like to make really important movies, like American Beauty. I was really proud to be a part of that movie.

Ally Condie
The beauty of dystopia is that it lets us vicariously experience future worlds - but we still have the power to change our own.

Amanda Peet
Beauty is only skin deep. If you go after someone just because she's beautiful but don't have anything to talk about, it's going to get boring fast. You want to look beyond the surface and see if you can have fun or if you have anything in common with this person.

Ambrose Bierce
Beauty, n: the power by which a woman charms a lover and terrifies a husband.

Ambrose Philips
The flowers anew, returning seasons bring but beauty faded has no second spring.

America Ferrera
I just wanted to see every single musical I could. The very first one I saw was 'Beauty and the Beast,' the only one I could get tickets for, and then 'Les Miserables' and then 'Chicago.'

Andre Breton
Beauty will be convulsive or will not be at all.

Andrea Jung
Avon invented the concept of direct marketing and direct selling beauty. And that's still very valid to us. We'll have a firm that will be around for another 114 years as strongly as it was the first 114.

———

A representative is free delivery she's a personal beauty consultant. Some people want that high touch.

———

The game in beauty is changing so much, if your product isn't high tech or can't make a unique performance claim - plump your lips, reduce your lines, look glossy, and stay on for 24 hours - you can't go to market today. I'm not just talking about a $20 lipstick, but a $5 lipstick!

Andrej Pejic
Fashion is quite inclusive and good at embracing different things and different forms of beauty. It's a very liberal industry. You can be yourself. Just not overweight.

Andrew Weil
A beautiful bouquet or a long-lasting flowering plant is a traditional gift for women, but I have recommended that both men and women keep fresh flowers in the home for their beauty, fragrance, and the lift they give our spirits.

Ani DiFranco
Sometimes the beauty is easy. Sometimes you don't have to try at all. Sometimes you can hear the wind blow in a handshake. Sometimes there's poetry written right on the bathroom wall.

Ann Curry
Beauty doesn't matter because in the end, we all lose our looks and all we have is our heart.

Anna Katharine Green
Hath the spirit of all beauty Kissed you in the path of duty?

––––––

There are two kinds of artists in this world those that work because the spirit is in them, and they cannot be silent if they would, and those that speak from a conscientious desire to make apparent to others the beauty that has awakened their own admiration.

Anna Quindlen
There is little premium in poetry in a world that thinks of Pound and Whitman as a weight and a sampler, not an Ezra, a Walt, a thing of beauty, a joy forever.

Anne Boyd
But I fear, my lot being cast in Scotland, that beauty would not be content.

Anne Frank
Think of all the beauty still left around you and be happy.

––––––

I don't think of all the misery but of the beauty that still remains.

Anne Lamott

If you don't die of thirst, there are blessings in the desert. You can be pulled into limitlessness, which we all yearn for, or you can do the beauty of minutiae, the scrimshaw of tiny and precise. The sky is your ocean, and the crystal silence will uplift you like great gospel music, or Neil Young.

———

Pay attention to the beauty surrounding you.

Anne Morrow Lindbergh

I have been overcome by the beauty and richness of our life together, those early mornings setting out, those evenings gleaming with rivers and lakes below us, still holding the last light.

Anne Roiphe

A woman whose smile is open and whose expression is glad has a kind of beauty no matter what she wears.

Annie Dillard

As soon as beauty is sought not from religion and love, but for pleasure, it degrades the seeker.

Annie Lennox

Most women are dissatisfied with their appearance - it's the stuff that fuels the beauty and fashion industries.

———

When I look at the majority of my own songs they really came from my own sense of personal confusion or need to express some pain or beauty - they were coming from a universal and personal place.

Anthony Kiedis

It seems like the chaos of this world is accelerating, but so is the beauty in the consciousness of more and more people.

Aristotle
Personal beauty is a greater recommendation than any letter of reference.

Arne Jacobsen
Proportions are what makes the old Greek temples classic in their beauty. They are like huge blocks, from which the air has been literally hewn out between the columns.

Arthur Cayley
As for everything else, so for a mathematical theory: beauty can be perceived but not explained.

Arthur Erickson
Only when inspired to go beyond consciousness by some extraordinary insight does beauty manifest unexpectedly.

Ashley Benson
My beauty icon is Angelina Jolie.

Ashley Smith
Life is full of beauty. Notice it. Notice the bumble bee, the small child, and the smiling faces. Smell the rain, and feel the wind. Live your life to the fullest potential, and fight for your dreams.

Auguste Renoir
The pain passes, but the beauty remains.

Bailey
The beautiful are never desolate, but someone always loves them.

Bar Refaeli
My mum is my beauty icon, because she represents what I think beauty is.

———

My everyday job is about superficial beauty, but when I'm not working I prefer to work on my inner beauty - I read a lot, I try to learn.

Baruch Spinoza
I would warn you that I do not attribute to nature either beauty or deformity, order or confusion. Only in relation to our imagination can things be called beautiful or ugly, well-ordered or confused.

Ben Okri
I am not fighting for success, just to get more beauty out of myself and share it with more people.

Benedict Spinoza
I would warn you that I do not attribute to nature either beauty or deformity, order or confusion. Only in relation to our imagination can things be called beautiful or ugly, well-ordered or confused.

Benjamin Franklin
Beauty and folly are old companions.

Bertrand Russell
Philosophy cannot itself determine the ends of life, but it can free us from the tyranny of prejudice and from distortions due to a narrow view. Love, beauty, knowledge, and joy in life; these things retain their lustre however wide our review. And if philosophy can help us to feel the value of these things, it will have played its part in man's collective work of bringing light into a world of darkness.

Beth Ditto
I thought to be feminine was to give in to straight culture, or the beauty standard, but in my heart I had a flair for fashion and style. They were passions I kept secret because I didn't understand I could love clothes and hair and makeup and still like girls.

———

Thanks to capitalism, the importance placed on beauty has never been so manipulated. We are the guinea pigs force-fed ads that tell us how pathetic we are: that we will never be loved, happy or valuable unless we have the body, the face, the hair, even the personality that will apparently be ours, if only we buy their products.

Beyonce Knowles
If I weren't performing, I'd be a beauty editor or a therapist. I love creativity, but I also love to help others. My mother was a hairstylist, and they listen to everyone's problems - like a beauty therapist!

Bill Griffith
I guess if you take yourself seriously as an artist there starts either the problem or the beauty of doing good artwork.

Bill Vaughan
Someday there is going to be a book about a middle-aged man with a good job, a beautiful wife and two lovely children who still manages to be happy.

Billie Joe Armstrong
A lot of punk rock is not going to be in the mainstream. It's below the radar. The beauty of it is that you're not supposed to always know. It's subterranean.

Billy Ocean
Suddenly life has new meaning to me, there's beauty up above and things we never take notice of, you wake up suddenly you're in love.

Blaise Pascal
Imagination disposes of everything it creates beauty, justice, and happiness, which are everything in this world.

Bob Dylan
I define nothing. Not beauty, not patriotism. I take each thing as it is, without prior rules about what it should be.

Boris Pasternak
You fall into my arms. You are the good gift of destruction's path, When life sickens more than disease. And boldness is the root of beauty. Which draws us together.

———

I don't like people who have never fallen or stumbled. Their virtue is lifeless and of little value. Life hasn't revealed its beauty to them.

Brad Meltzer
Stories aren't the beauty of what did happen. They're the beauty of what could happen.

Brigitte Bardot
I gave my beauty and my youth to men. I am going to give my wisdom and experience to animals.

Brooke Burke
Power and beauty come from a very deep place.

Bryant McGill
Seek goodness and be goodness. Seek beauty and be beauty. Seek love and be love.

Buddy Holly
I'm not trying to stump anybody... it's the beauty of the language that I'm interested in.

Busy Philipps
After 'Freaks and Geeks,' I dealt with several producers who wanted to cover up all my beauty marks, every single mole on my body. They tried to cover them on my first two episodes of 'Dawson's Creek,' and it just looked ridiculous, so I had to put my foot down. But it's not something I'm insecure about.

Camille Paglia

The 1990s, after the reign of terror of academic vandalism, will be a decade of restoration: restoration of meaning, value, beauty, pleasure, and emotion to art and restoration of art to its audience.

———

Younger women have no problem in reconciling beauty with ambitions as a professional woman.

Candice Bergen

Beauty set up distance between other people and me. It warped their behavior.

———

People see you as an object, not as a person, and they project a set of expectations onto you. People who don't have it think beauty is a blessing, but actually it sets you apart.

Candice Swanepoel

I was always interested in fashion and beauty. I was fifteen when I was scouted in a flea market. Two years later, I arrived in New York. I was in awe because it was like another planet.

Carl Van Vechten

As an inspiration to the author, I do not think the cat can be over-estimated. He suggests so much grace, power, beauty, motion, mysticism. I do not wonder that many writers love cats I am only surprised that all do not.

Carol Alt

I am thrilled to be able to bring my vision of beauty to others who may be inspired by it.

Carre Otis

We come in many different shapes and sizes, and we need to support each other and our differences. Our beauty is in our differences.

———

I'm proud that today, at 43 years old, I've come to value the aging process and focus on inner rather than outer beauty.

Cat Stevens
This is the beauty of the Qur'an: it asks you to reflect and reason, and not to worship the sun or moon but the One who has created everything. The Qur'an asks man to reflect upon the sun and moon and God's creation in general.

Cate Blanchett
My everyday beauty routine is always rushed and pretty simple.

———

Well, I've never looked upon myself as being a beauty, per se.

Celine Dion
There's no such thing is aging, but maturing and knowledge. It's beautiful, I call that beauty.

Luis Cernuda
Everything beautiful has its moment and then passes away.

Chaim Potok
Every man who has shown the world the way to beauty, to true culture, has been a rebel, a 'universal' without patriotism, without home, who has found his people everywhere.

Chanakya
The world's biggest power is the youth and beauty of a woman.

Charles Baudelaire
Whether you come from heaven or hell, what does it matter, O Beauty!

———

The pleasure we derive from the representation of the present is due, not only to the beauty it can be clothed in, but also to its essential quality of being the present.

———

There are as many kinds of beauty as there are habitual ways of seeking happiness.

———

The study of beauty is a duel in which the artist cries with terror before being defeated.

Beauty is the sole ambition, the exclusive goal of Taste.

———

To copy beauty forfeits all pretense to fame to copy faults is want of sense.

Charles Kingsley
Never lose an opportunity of seeing anything beautiful, for beauty is God's handwriting.

Charles Lamb
Let us live for the beauty of our own reality.

Charles Reade
Beauty is power; a smile is its sword.

Charlie Chaplin
I do not have much patience with a thing of beauty that must be explained to be understood. If it does need additional interpretation by someone other than the creator, then I question whether it has fulfilled its purpose.

Charlie Haden
I just try to play music from my heart and bring as much beauty as I can to as many people as I can. Just give them other alternatives, especially people who aren't exposed to creative music.

———

We're here to bring beauty to the world and make a difference in this planet. That's what art forms are about.

Charlotte Smith
The cottage garden most for use designed, Yet not of beauty destitute.

Cheryl Tiegs
I've been on the cover of 'Time' magazine three times, not for my beauty but because what I was doing was newsworthy around the world. I've worked with teams all my life, but I've been nice and I've been kind.

Chita Rivera
Beauty is not everything!

Christina Aguilera
Blues and soul and jazz music has so much pain, so much beauty of raw emotion and passion.

Christina Rossetti
She gave up beauty in her tender youth, gave all her hope and joy and pleasant ways she covered up her eyes lest they should gaze on vanity, and chose the bitter truth.

Christo
We tell them that we believe it will be beautiful because that is our specialty, we only create joy and beauty. We have never done a sad work. Through the drawings, we hope a majority will be able to visualize it.

_____

And for me, the real world involves everything: risk, danger, beauty, energy, all we meet with in the real world.

Christopher Lambert
Acting is still, of course, what I love to do most. The beauty of it is that by changing characters, it never gets boring.

Christopher McCandless
Tramping is too easy with all this money. My days were more exciting when I was penniless and had to forage around for my next meal... I've decided that I'm going to live this life for some time to come. The freedom and simple beauty of it is just too good to pass up.

Christopher Meloni
My wife has brought great beauty into my life. And my daughter has brought me nothing but joy. Those qualities were greatly lacking.

Christopher Morley
Beauty is ever to the lonely mind a shadow fleeting she is never plain. She is a visitor who leaves behind the gift of grief, the souvenir of pain.

_____

In every man's heart there is a secret nerve that answers to the vibrations of beauty.

_____

All cities are mad: but the madness is gallant. All cities are beautiful: but the beauty is grim.

Christopher Wren
In things to be seen at once, much variety makes confusion, another vice of beauty. In things that are not seen at once, and have no respect one to another, great variety is commendable, provided this variety transgress not the rules of optics and geometry.

Christy Turlington
When you are balanced and when you listen and attend to the needs of your body, mind, and spirit, your natural beauty comes out.

Cindy Margolis
Having inner beauty is something you develop on your own, and I like to think I have that.

Clarence Stein
A small house must depend on its grouping with other houses for its beauty, and for the preservation of light air and the maximum of surrounding open space.

Claude Debussy
Beauty must appeal to the senses, must provide us with immediate enjoyment, must impress us or insinuate itself into us without any effort on our part.

Clifford Geertz
The way in which mathematicians and physicists and historians talk is quite different, and what a physicist means by physical intuition and what a mathematician means by beauty or elegance are things worth thinking about.

Colin Quinn
That's the beauty of being a comedian - it's the one job you're allowed to do that. We're lucky. We're really lucky.

Colleen Atwood
Knowing who the actors were as you were designing them helped, with Catherine's beauty and Renee's frailty, they directed me visually just by who they were.

Colton
Pleasure is to Women what the Sun is to the Flower; if moderately enjoyed, it beautifies, it refreshes, and it improves; if immoderately, it withers, etiolates, and destroys.

Confucius
Everything has beauty, but not everyone sees it.

Conor Oberst
If the world could remain within a frame like a painting on the wall, I think we'd see the beauty then and stand staring in awe.

Conrad Hall
There is a kind of beauty in imperfection.

Countess of Blessington
There is no cosmetic for beauty like happiness.

Courtney Love
I don't need plastic in my body to validate me as a woman.

Craig Bruce
Nothing surpasses the beauty and elegance of a bad idea.

Craig Ferguson
It's the beauty and curse of doing a daily show. Some days you've got nothing to talk about and other days Dick Cheney shoots his lawyer in the face and everyone is happy.

Cristina Saralegui
Latin life is rich with warmth, family values and history. I want to bring that beauty into American homes.

Dame Edith Evans
What I want to give in the theatre is beauty, that's what I want to give.

Dan Hawkins
You can muck around with different guitars for certain bits, but you have to have your own sound. That's your benchmark, that's your sound. I also play a Black Beauty. It sounds amazing.

Danica McKellar
It's such a diversion to be constantly thinking of better ways I can teach people math that my hunger is for that really, for new ways of translating the beauty of it.

Danny Elfman
The beauty of a main title is that you establish your main theme and maybe a bit of your secondary theme. You plant the seed that you're going to go water later in the score. And so, having that removed just made it so much more difficult.

Dante Alighieri
Beauty awakens the soul to act.

Dante Alighieri
Heat cannot be separated from fire, or beauty from The Eternal.

Daphne Zuniga
You don't have to save the world, but you can be in the world-that's where the beauty comes from.

Dave Brubeck
That's the beauty of music. You can take a theme from a Bach sacred chorale and improvise. It doesn't make any difference where the theme comes from the treatment of it can be jazz.

Dave Grohl
Through Kurt I saw the beauty of minimalism and the importance of music that's stripped down.

David Allan Coe
It is not the beauty of a building you should look at its the construction of the foundation that will stand the test of time.

David Amram
We had common interests in the beauty of the French language. We both had a tremendous love of jazz. We shared dreams of getting married and having a family, living in the country, leading an idyllic life.

David Attenborough
It seems to me that the natural world is the greatest source of excitement the greatest source of visual beauty the greatest source of intellectual interest. It is the greatest source of so much in life that makes life worth living.

David Gower
The double hundred Fowler hit in the Madras Test was an absolute beauty.

David Hume
Beauty in things exists in the mind which contemplates them.

———

Beauty, whether moral or natural, is felt, more properly than perceived.

———

Accuracy is, in every case, advantageous to beauty, and just reasoning to delicate sentiment. In vain would we exalt the one by depreciating the other.

David Remnick
The world is a crazy, beautiful, ugly complicated place, and it keeps moving on from crisis to strangeness to beauty to weirdness to tragedy. The caravan keeps moving on, and the job of the longform writer or filmmaker or radio broadcaster is to stop - is to pause - and when the caravan goes away, that's when this stuff comes.

David Rittenhouse
For the greater beauty of the instrument, the balls representing the planets are to be of considerable bigness but so contrived, that they may be taken off at pleasure, and others, much smaller, and fitter for some purposes, put in their places.

Delta Burke
Blanche talks about aging, and why should she be considered poor, because physical beauty is transitory and fading and she has such richness of the soul. I think that speech is so beautiful, and so telling and so true.

Dennis Prager
Our scientific age demands that we provide definitions, measurements, and statistics in order to be taken seriously. Yet most of the important things in life cannot be precisely defined or measured. Can we define or measure love, beauty, friendship, or decency, for example?

Derek Walcott
Visual surprise is natural in the Caribbean it comes with the landscape, and faced with its beauty, the sigh of History dissolves.

Diane Kruger
Her beauty didn't do her any good and she couldn't use it in any positive way or manipulative way. I just hope that people will look and see and believe in that hope of love, that hope of freedom, even if it was just for a limited time.

_____

I'm not one of those women who thinks beauty is a curse.

_____

A lot of directors idealize their leading ladies or turn them into these objects of sexuality and beauty.

_____

I like the idea of accessibility, coming from a lower-middle-class background myself, I feel like beauty and products should be accessible to all women over the world.

Dita Von Teese
I think the beauty looks I most regret are those I was persuaded into.

___

Physical beauty isn't so impressive to me.

___

My beauty icons are women whose images are self-created.

___

I really believe that beauty comes from health - sensible eating and exercise.

Dodie Smith
Time takes the ugliness and horror out of death and turns it into beauty.

Don DeLillo
I felt Joyce was an influence on my fiction, but in a very general way, as a kind of inspiration and a model for the beauty of language.

Donald Knuth
Everyday life is like programming, I guess. If you love something you can put beauty into it.

Donald Norman
Beauty and brains, pleasure and usability - they should go hand in hand.

Donna Rice
Shortly thereafter, some friends encouraged me to try out for the Miss South Carolina World beauty pageant. To my surprise, I won - and was sent to New York City to compete nationally.

Doris Day
Well I do find the beauty in animals. I find beauty everywhere. I find beauty in my garden.

Douglas Horton
Beauty is variable, ugliness is constant.

Douglas Sirk
In the 19th century, you had bourgeois art without politics - an almost frozen idea of what beauty is.

Duchess of Windsor
It is good that the young are beautiful; it is the only advantage they have.

E.B. White
Is there anything in the universe more beautiful and protective than the simple complexity of a spider's web?

Eartha Kitt
Aging has a wonderful beauty and we should have respect for that.

Ed Rendell
One of the things that people don't realize is that that natural beauty, those recreational forests, they have an economic development impact for the state as well.

Edgar Rice Burroghs
It never seems to occur to some people, that, like beauty, a sense of humor may sometimes be fatal.

Edmund Burke
Beauty is the promise of happiness.

Edward Garrett
The vain beauty cares most for the conquest which employed the whole artillery of her charms.

Edward Gibbon
Beauty is an outward gift which is seldom despised, except by those to whom it has been refused.

Edward James Olmos
You get more churches burned down in the United States in the last two years than in the last hundred, because of the lack of understanding of culture and diversity and the beauty of it.

Edward Robert Bulwer-Lytton
In life, as in art, the beautiful moves in curves.

Edward Witten
But the beauty of Einstein's equations, for example, is just as real to anyone who's experienced it as the beauty of music. We've learned in the 20th century that the equations that work have inner harmony.

———

One of the basic things about a string is that it can vibrate in many different shapes or forms, which gives music its beauty.

Edwin Way Teale
For the mind disturbed, the still beauty of dawn is nature's finest balm.

Elisabeth Kubler-Ross
People are like stained - glass windows. They sparkle and shine when the sun is out, but when the darkness sets in, their true beauty is revealed only if there is a light from within.

Eliza Farnham
The human face is the organic seat of beauty. It is the register of value in development, a record of Experience, whose legitimate office is to perfect the life, a legible language to those who will study it, of the majestic mistress, the soul.

Elizabeth Arden
Hold fast to youth and beauty.

Elizabeth Barrett Browning
The beautiful seems right by force of beauty and the feeble wrong because of weakness.

Ella R. Bloor
I think Whitman more than any other poet possessed the gift of revealing to others the beauty of everything around us, the beauty of nature, the beauty of human beings.

Ellen Page
As a girl, you're supposed to love Sleeping Beauty. I mean, who wants to love Sleeping Beauty when you can be Aladdin?

Elliott Erwitt
I appreciate simplicity, true beauty that lasts over time, and a little wit and eclecticism that make life more fun.

Emily Dickinson
Beauty is not caused. It is.

Emily Mortimer
Los Angeles is like a beauty parlor at the end of the universe.

Emily Prager
Beauty is the still birth of suffering, every woman knows that.

Emmanuelle Beart
Beauty is not something you can count on. Usually, when people say you are beautiful, it is when there is a harmony between the inside and the outside.

Emmanuelle Chriqui
The beauty of voice-over work is that maybe you come in and record once every two weeks for a couple of hours and do a couple episodes a session. It's awesome! You spend an afternoon playing in the booth, and there you have it. It doesn't interfere with much.

_____

My mom was an aesthetician and she went to beauty school back in the '60s. I just remember watching her do her makeup all the time. She always had her nails done, makeup on - her face was ready to go when she went out. I loved it.

Erasmus
Love that has nothing but beauty to keep it in good health is short lived, and apt to have ague fits.

Eric Bana
I think the beauty of working with young people is they remind you of the spirit of acting and it's just a big play.

Eric Davis
I love the game, it's the greatest game on earth, that's why I can't understand all of this talk about trying to make the game better. People talk about the high strike zone and changing this and that. Why? To speed up the game? That's the beauty of baseball. There is no time element.

Erica Durance
The best beauty advice I ever received is to keep skin hydrated and limit harsh exposure to the sun. If you are set on the tanned look, there are plenty of great creams that will give you a healthy-looking glow.

_____

I maintain my inner beauty by trying to lead a balanced life in general. I try to eat healthy foods, but... that doesn't mean I won't treat myself now and then! I work out almost every day, which gives me more energy and helps me feel stronger. I also try to be a genuinely good person to the people around me.

Erika Slezak
And at five o'clock in the morning we left to drive to Old Tucson, and I sat with my mouth open in the van. I was stunned by the beauty of that country.

Ernst Haas
All I wanted was to connect my moods with those of Paris. Beauty paints and when it painted most, I shot.

Eugene Ionesco
Beauty is a precious trace that eternity causes to appear to us and that it takes away from us. A manifestation of eternity, and a sign of death as well.

Eugene Ormandy
Beauty is less important than quality.

Eva Herzigova
Italian men do appreciate beautiful women. They're not afraid of the beauty, which is nice.

Evangeline Lilly
I'm from Canada, and New Zealand feels like you took all the best bits of Canada and squished them onto a tiny island like Hawaii. I was absolutely blown away by the beauty of the South Island.

Evelyn Underhill
All things are perceived in the light of charity, and hence under the aspect of beauty for beauty is simply reality seen with the eyes of love.

F. Scott Fitzgerald
It was only a sunny smile, and little it cost in the giving, but like morning light it scattered the night and made the day worth living.

Faith Hill
I think beauty comes from within. If you're happy and look at life in the best way you can, even when there are problems, it can make you beautiful on the outside.

Fanny Brice
Personal beauty is a greater recommendation than any letter of reference.

Farrah Fawcett
The reason that the all-American boy prefers beauty to brains is that he can see better than he can think.

Felicity Huffman
I look OK. I look better in person than I do on film, which is bad because it's how I make my living, but I am not a beauty and on balance I am glad.

Beauty can make you powerful in a way that isn't good for you. Being OK is better for the person I have become.

Florence King
Americans worship creativity the way they worship physical beauty - as a way of enjoying elitism without guilt: God did it.

Florenz Ziegfeld
Beauty, of course, is the most important requirement and the paramount asset of the applicant.

Francesca da Rimini
Search for beauty without features, something deeper than any signs.

Francine Pascal
When I first thought of the idea for 'Sweet Valley High,' I loved the idea of high school as microcosm of the real world. And what I really liked was how it moved things on from 'Sleeping Beauty'-esque romance novels where the girl had to wait for the hero. This would be girl-driven, very different, I decided - and indeed it is.

Francis Bacon
Beauty itself is but the sensible image of the Infinite.

———

There is no excellent beauty that hath not some strangeness in the proportion.

———

Beauty is as summer fruits, which are easy to corrupt and cannot last; and for the most part it makes a dissolute youth, and an age a little out of countenance; but if it light well, it makes virtue shine and vice blush.

———

The best part of beauty is that which no picture can express.

Frank Miller
Comics are so full of amazing work. And I can't look at a drawing of a woman without thinking of, for instance, Wallace Wood and his amazing way of capturing beauty.

Frank Norris
Truth is a thing immortal and perpetual, and it gives to us a beauty that fades not away in time.

Franz Kafka
Youth is happy because it has the ability to see beauty. Anyone who keeps the ability to see beauty never grows old.

Frederick Sanger
When I was young my Father used to tell me that the two most worthwhile pursuits in life were the pursuit of truth and of beauty and I believe that Alfred Nobel must have felt much the same when he gave these prizes for literature and the sciences.

Friedrich Schiller
The key to education is the experience of beauty.

Fritz Todt
The ever increasing spiritual damage caused by life within the big city will make this hunger practically uncontrollable when we build here on this the landscape of our homeland we must be clear that we will protect its beauty.

———

In places where this beauty has already disappeared, we will reconstruct it.

Gabrielle Union
Hollywood needs to recognise all shades of African American beauty.

Gail Simmons
I cannot go to Montreal without going to Beauty's, my favorite place for breakfast, where I have the Mish-Mash omelet with hot dogs, salami, eggs, green peppers, and onions, and the best banana bread in the world. It's legendary!

Gaston Bachelard
A special kind of beauty exists which is born in language, of language, and for language.

Gene Tierney
Wealth, beauty, and fame are transient. When those are gone, little is left except the need to be useful.

Georg Brandes
But when I was twelve years old I caught my first strong glimpse of one of the fundamental forces of existence, whose votary I was destined to be for life - namely, Beauty.

Georg Wilhelm Friedrich Hegel
I'm not ugly, but my beauty is a total creation.

George Bancroft
Beauty is but the sensible image of the Infinite. Like truth and justice it lives within us like virtue and the moral law it is a companion of the soul.

George Bernard Shaw
Beauty is all very well at first sight but who ever looks at it when it has been in the house three days?

George Chapman
Let no man value at a little price a virtuous woman's counsel; her winged spirit is feathered often times with heavenly words, and, like her beauty, ravishing and pure.

George Byron
I slept and dreamt that life was beauty I woke and found that life was duty.

George Edward Moore
Faith goes out through the window when beauty comes in at the door.

George Eliot
It seems to me we can never give up longing and wishing while we are thoroughly alive. There are certain things we feel to be beautiful and good, and we must hunger after them.

George H. Mead
The beauty of a face is not a separate quality but a relation or proportion of qualities to each other.

George Henry Lewes
Endeavour to be faithful, and if there is any beauty in your thought, your style will be beautiful if there is any real emotion to express, the expression will be moving.

George Henry Lewes
Many a genius has been slow of growth. Oaks that flourish for a thousand years do not spring up into beauty like a reed.

George Meredith
A witty woman is a treasure a witty beauty is a power.

George Sand
The beauty that addresses itself to the eyes is only the spell of the moment the eye of the body is not always that of the soul.

George Saunders
I still believe that capitalism is too harsh and I believe that, even within that, there is a lot of satisfaction and beauty if you happen to be one of the lucky ones, although that doesn't eradicate the reality of the suffering. It's all true at once, kind of humming and sublime.

Geraldine Brooks
I mean the beauty of being a writer is it's not like being a swimmer. When they were talking about our Olympic swimmers and they'd say, 'Oh she's so old,' and she's all of 25 or something. So the beauty for a writer is that you can keep doing it right into your dotage, and I hope to be able to keep doing it as long as I can get away with it, yeah.

Gerard Butler
I was amazed and upset by the looks I got just walking around the studio... It illuminates the ugliness and the beauty that exists within each of us, and that's what this story represents to me.

Gerard Manley Hopkins
Beauty is a relation, and the apprehension of it a comparison.

Gian Carlo Menotti
Art is the unceasing effort to compete with the beauty of flowers - and never succeeding.

Giuseppe Garibaldi
You, too, women, cast away all the cowards from your embraces they will give you only cowards for children, and you who are the daughters of the land of beauty must bear children who are noble and brave.

Godfrey Harold Hardy
Beauty is the first test: there is no permanent place in the world for ugly mathematics.

Goldwin Smith
Every one who has a heart, however ignorant of architecture he may be, feels the transcendent beauty and poetry of the mediaeval churches.

Gordon Gee
The arts, quite simply, nourish the soul. They sustain, comfort, inspire. There is nothing like that exquisite moment when you first discover the beauty of connecting with others in celebration of larger ideals and shared wisdom.

Gotthold Ephraim Lessing
For me the greatest beauty always lies in the greatest clarity.

Grant-Lee Phillips
I played with the same band for years and years and there's a beauty to having one solid core that you keep exploring. On the other hand, it's nice to throw yourself in different situations where you find out things about your own resources.

George Grenville
The criterion of true beauty is, that it increases in examination; of false, that it lessens. There is something, therefore, in true beauty that corresponds with the right reason, and it is not merely the creature of fancy.

Groucho Marx
She got her looks from her father. He's a plastic surgeon.

Guglielmo Marconi
You will also allow me to thank the Academy for inviting me to lecture in Stockholm, for its hospitality, and for the opportunity afforded me for admiring the charm of your people and the beauty of your country.

Gustav Mahler
Beauty and fullness of tone can be achieved by having the whole orchestra play with high clarinets and a carefully selected number of piccolos.

Gustav Stickley
There are elements of intrinsic beauty in the simplification of a house built on the log cabin idea.

———

First, there is the bare beauty of the logs themselves with their long lines and firm curves. Then there is the open charm felt of the structural features which are not hidden under plaster and ornament, but are clearly revealed, a charm felt in Japanese architecture.

Gustav Stresemann
The concept of active cooperation has taken the place of opposition to the new form of government and of dreamy resignation entranced with the beauty of times past.

Gustave Courbet
The expression of beauty is in direct ratio to the power of conception the artist has acquired.

Beauty, like truth, is relative to the time when one lives and to the individual who can grasp it. The expression of beauty is in direct ratio to the power of conception the artist has acquired.

Gwyneth Paltrow
Beauty, to me is about being comfortable in your own skin.

H. G. Wells
Beauty is in the heart of the beholder.

Halle Berry
Let me tell you something - being thought of as a beautiful woman has spared me nothing in life. No heartache, no trouble. Love has been difficult. Beauty is essentially meaningless and it is always transitory.

_____

I think we have become obsessed with beauty and personally I'm really saddened by the way women mutilate their faces today in search of that.

Hannah Arendt
By its very nature the beautiful is isolated from everything else. From beauty no road leads to reality.

Hans Urs von Balthasar
Our situation today shows that beauty demands for itself at least as much courage and decision as do truth and goodness, and she will not allow herself to be separated and banned from her two sisters without taking them along with herself in an act of mysterious vengeance.

_____

Not longer loved or fostered by religion, beauty is lifted from its face as a mask, and its absence exposes features on that face which threaten to become incomprehensible to man.

_____

We no longer dare to believe in beauty and we make of it a mere appearance in order the more easily to dispose of it.

_____

It is, finally, a word is untimely in three different senses, and bearing it as one's treasure will not win one anyone's favours one rather risks finding oneself outside everyone's camp... Beauty is the word that shall be our first.

Harold Hamm
It's harder, but we're still finding oil in Oklahoma today. The bar has been raised on startup companies, but it can still be done. Every regulation and every rule limits you, but, yes, it can still be done. That's the beauty of living in a free country and having the freedom to have an idea and become an entrepreneur.

Harriet Beecher Stowe
So much has been said and sung of beautiful young girls, why doesn't somebody wake up to the beauty of old women.

Havelock Ellis
The absence of flaw in beauty is itself a flaw.

Hayden Panettiere
I remember reminding myself that beauty is an opinion, not a fact. And it has always made me feel better.

Heather Kozar
I feel by posing for Playboy I've discovered my own sexuality and beauty, and I feel more confident than ever.

Heather Wilson
We need a balanced, long term energy policy to reduce our dependence on foreign oil and preserve the beauty of the land we love.

Hector Hugh Munro
I always say beauty is only sin deep.

Helen Gurley Brown
Beauty can't amuse you, but brainwork - reading, writing, thinking - can.

Helen Rowland
A bachelor never quite gets over the idea that he is a thing of beauty and a boy forever.

_____

Helen Rowland
Somehow a bachelor never quite gets over the idea that he is a thing of beauty and a boy forever.

Helena Christensen
The more people explore the world, the more they realize in every country there's a different aesthetic. Beauty really is in the eye of the beholder.

_____

There will always be a desire for something new, fresh and innovative, as well as a yearning and respect for timeless elegance and beauty.

Helmut Jahn
You don't know what the Chinese expect in the way of beauty. The presentation is just a farce. You come into a room filled with 50 people and they don't talk to you. There's very little interaction.

Henry David Thoreau

It's the beauty within us that makes it possible for us to recognize the beauty around us. The question is not what you look at but what you see.

___

It is something to be able to paint a particular picture, or to carve a statue, and so to make a few objects beautiful; but it is far more glorious to carve and paint the very atmosphere and medium through which we look, which morally we can do. To affect the quality of the day, that is the highest of arts.

Henry Drummond
Strength of character may be learned at work, but beauty of character is learned at home.

Henry James
In art economy is always beauty.

Herbert Gold
Literature boils with the madcap careers of writers brought to the edge by the demands of living on their nerves, wringing out their memories and their nightmares to extract meaning, truth, beauty.

Herbie Hancock
I think there's a great beauty to having problems. That's one of the ways we learn.

Homer
In youth and beauty, wisdom is but rare!

Horace
Nothing's beautiful from every point of view.

Howard Carter
We were astonished by the beauty and refinement of the art displayed by the objects surpassing all we could have imagined - the impression was overwhelming.

Howard Lindsay
I shall give you hunger, and pain, and sleepless nights. Also beauty, and satisfactions known to few, and glimpses of the heavenly life. None of these you shall have continually, and of their coming and going you shall not be foretold.

Hu Shih
What is sacred among one people may be ridiculous in another and what is despised or rejected by one cultural group, may in a different environment become the cornerstone for a great edifice of strange grandeur and beauty.

Hugh Hefner
The difference between Marilyn Monroe and the early Pamela Anderson is not that great. What's amazing is that the taste of American men and international tastes in terms of beauty have essentially stayed the same. Styles change, but our view of beauty stays the same.

Hugh Jackman
The first show I ever did, singing and dancing, was 'Beauty and the Beast.' I was playing Gaston. Gaston has red tights, knee high boots, and it's very physical. I had headaches every day for two months.

Ian Rush
This is why cup finals are so special because on the day anyone can beat anyone. That's what it's all about and that's why for me the FA Cup and the Carling Cup are the best cups in the world. That's the beauty of the cup.

Idina Menzel
As a mom, I don't have much time for beauty.

Irving Washington
After all, it is the divinity within that makes the divinity without and I have been more fascinated by a woman of talent and intelligence, though deficient in personal charms, than I have been by the most regular beauty.

Isaac Albeniz
I want the Arabic Granada, that which is art, which is all that seems to me beauty and emotion.

Isidore Ducasse Lautreamont
Throughout the centuries, man has considered himself beautiful. I rather suppose that man only believes in his own beauty out of pride that he is not really beautiful and he suspects this himself for why does he look on the face of his fellow-man with such scorn?

Jack London
I write for no other purpose than to add to the beauty that now belongs to me. I write a book for no other reason than to add three or four hundred acres to my magnificent estate.

Jacqueline Bisset
A mode of conduct, a standard of courage, discipline, fortitude and integrity can do a great deal to make a woman beautiful.

―――

I am a great lover of art, in many forms: paintings, objets, textiles. I don't have the talent for painting, but I have a very good sense of colour, a love of visual beauty.

James Baldwin
The South is very beautiful but its beauty makes one sad because the lives that people live here, and have lived here, are so ugly.

James Beattie
And beauty immortal awakes from the tomb.

James De La Vega
Beauty magazines make my girlfriend feel ugly.

James Dyson
Beauty can come in strange forms.

James Hillman
Depression opens the door to beauty of some kind.

James Matthew Barrie
It's a sort of bloom on a woman. If you have it you don't need to have anything else; and if you don't have it, it doesn't much matter what else you have.

James Nasmyth
But my most favourite pursuit, after my daily exertions at the Foundry, was Astronomy. There were frequently clear nights when the glorious objects in the Heavens were seen in most attractive beauty and brilliancy.

James Randolph Adams
Great designers seldom make great advertising men, because they get overcome by the beauty of the picture - and forget that merchandise must be sold.

James Russell Lowell
Every man feels instinctively that all the beautiful sentiments in the world weigh less than a single lovely action.

James Thomson
I know no subject more elevating, more amazing, more ready to the poetical enthusiasm, the philosophical reflection, and the moral sentiment than the works of nature. Where can we meet such variety, such beauty, such magnificence?

James Weldon Johnson
I thought of Paris as a beauty spot on the face of the earth, and of London as a big freckle.

James Wolcott
After a decade this glum, we deserved a shot of 'Glee,' a show that restored our faith in the power of song, the beauty of dance, and the magic of 'spirit fingers' to chase our cares and woes into somebody else's backyard.

Jamie Zawinski
Of course, all of the software I write runs on Linux that's the beauty of standards, and of cross-platform code. I don't have to run your OS, and you don't have to run mine, and we can use the same applications anyway!

Jane Asher
Listening to my regular favourites - Mozart, Beethoven, Brahms and so on - I always feel, quite misguidedly, that nothing can be too bad if such beauty and brilliance exists in the world.

Jane Seymour
Beauty is a radiance that originates from within and comes from inner security and strong character.

Jane Smiley
I discovered that the horse is life itself, a metaphor but also an example of life's mystery and unpredictability, of life's generosity and beauty, a worthy object of repeated and ever changing contemplation.

Janelle Monae
I believe it's time that women truly owned their superpowers and used their beauty and strength to change the world around them.

Janelle Monae
Some songs you get. Some songs you may not. And I think that's the beauty of art: to question and to ask, to understand the deeper meaning after two or three or four listenings.

Janice Dickinson
Beauty opened all the doors it got me things I didn't even know I wanted, and things I certainly didn't deserve.

Janis Ian
I learned the truth at seventeen, That love was meant for beauty queens, And high school girls with clear skinned smiles, Who married young and then retired.

Jawaharlal Nehru
We live in a wonderful world that is full of beauty, charm and adventure. There is no end to the adventures that we can have if only we seek them with our eyes open.

Jean Genet
I recognize in thieves, traitors and murderers, in the ruthless and the cunning, a deep beauty - a sunken beauty.

Jean Kerr
I'm tired of all this nonsense about beauty being skin deep. That's deep enough. What do you want, an adorable pancreas?

Jean Paul
Beauty attracts us men but if, like an armed magnet it is pointed, beside, with gold and silver, it attracts with tenfold power.

Jean Paul
Whenever, at a party, I have been in the mood to study fools, I have always looked for a great beauty: they always gather round her like flies around a fruit stall.

Jean Paul Gaultier
I would like to say to people, open your eyes and find beauty where you normally don't expect it.

Jean Paul Richter
Beauty attracts us men; but if, like an armed magnet it is pointed, beside, with gold and silver, it attracts with tenfold power.

Jean Rostand
Beauty in art is often nothing but ugliness subdued.

Jean Toomer
No eyes that have seen beauty ever lose their sight.

Jean-Luc Godard
Beauty is composed of an eternal, invariable element whose quantity is extremely difficult to determine, and a relative element which might be, either by turns or all at once, period, fashion, moral, passion.

Jeanne Moreau
Beyond the beauty, the sex, the titillation, the surface, there is a human being. And that has to emerge.

Jeb Bush
Who among us has never looked up into the heavens on a starlit night, lost in wonder at the vastness of space and the beauty of the stars?

Jeff Vandermeer
I do believe very much in the idea of unexpected or 'convulsive' beauty - beauty in the service of liberty.

Jenifer Lewis
I don't have any beauty shop memories. I remember the barber shop.

Jenifer Lewis
We didn't have a beauty shop as I grew up.

Jennifer Aniston
I was always reading those beauty magazines and wanting to become this unattainable thing.

Jennifer Garner
Beauty comes from a life well lived. If you've lived well, your smile lines are in the right places, and your frown lines aren't too bad, what more do you need?

———

My mother is a big believer in being responsible for your own happiness. She always talked about finding joy in small moments and insisted that we stop and take in the beauty of an ordinary day. When I stop the car to make my kids really see a sunset, I hear my mother's voice and smile.

Jennifer Lopez
I don't get anything for free. I pay for all my beauty treatments.

Jerry Hall
Music, art, theater. I'm just a big fan of beauty.

Jerry Mathers
I have several computer companies. One of them I have a program for wide-format printing. I have a beauty program. So I have several different programs that I own for printing.

Jerry Saltz
I love Rauschenberg. I love that he created a turning point in visual history, that he redefined the idea of beauty, that he combined painting, sculpture, photography, and everyday life with such gall, and that he was interested in, as he put it, 'the ability to conceive failure as progress."

———

Abstraction brings the world into more complex, variable relations it can extract beauty, alternative topographies, ugliness, and intense actualities from seeming nothingness.

Jessica Ennis
My idea of beauty is somebody that doesn't have to try too much, someone who is effortless and fresh.

Joan Blondell
I don't know what the secret to longevity as an actress is. It's more than talent and beauty. Maybe it's the audience seeing itself in you.

Joan Chen
Beauty is the result of having been through an experience all the way through to the end - therefore it has a poignancy. Beauty that is singular always comes from following an experience to the point where you can go no further.

Joan Collins
The problem with beauty is that it's like being born rich and getting poorer.

———

And I think of that again as I've written in several of my beauty books, a lot of health comes from the proper eating habits, which are something that - you know, I come from a generation that wasn't - didn't have a lot of food.

Joan Crawford
I have always known what I wanted, and that was beauty... in every form.

Joan Rivers
The ideal beauty is a fugitive which is never found.

Joan Smalls
I just want to continue to break barriers and to show the industry and the world that beauty is diverse, and you don't have to be a certain stereotype to be beautiful.

Jock Sturges
Physical beauty is such a strange thing.

Jody Watley
There's one more thing I want to say. It's a touchy subject. Black beauty. Black sensuality. We live in a culture where the beauty of black people isn't always as celebrated as other types. I'd like to help change that if I can!

Joel McHale
In prison, inmates sometimes use Cheetos and grape juice as makeup. I wouldn't use that beauty regimen around Britney Spears - she might lick your face off!

Johann von Schiller
Truth exists for the wise, beauty for the feeling heart.

Johann Wolfgang von Goethe
The soul that sees beauty may sometimes walk alone.

———

Beauty is a manifestation of secret natural laws, which otherwise would have been hidden from us forever.

———

Beauty is everywhere a welcome guest.

John Cheever
For me, a page of good prose is where one hears the rain and the noise of battle. It has the power to give grief or universality that lends it a youthful beauty.

John Clayton
There is no racial or ethnic involvement in Thanksgiving, and people who may be very distant from the Christian system can see the beauty and the positive spirit that comes from the holiday.

John Derek
I think love and beauty are what life is all about.

John Donne
Love built on beauty, soon as beauty dies.

John Dryden
Beauty, like ice, our footing does betray; Who can tread sure on the smooth, slippery way: Pleased with the surface, we glide swiftly on, And see the dangers that we cannot shun.

John Erskine
There's a difference between beauty and charm. A beautiful woman is one I notice. A charming woman is one who notices me.

John Foster
The awesomeness of God is that even in the works of the Beach Boys, Beatles, etc., the beauty of the music is a mere reflection of what God does everyday. He creates music of all kinds and moods.

John Galsworthy
He was afflicted by the thought that where Beauty was, nothing ever ran quite straight, which no doubt, was why so many people looked on it as immoral.

John Greenleaf Whittier
Beauty seen is never lost, God's colors all are fast.

John Keats
A thing of beauty is a joy forever: its loveliness increases it will never pass into nothingness.

John Lone
The beauty of it is when you can just show up and hit the notes.

John Lubbock
There are three great questions which in life we have over and over again to answer: Is it right or wrong? Is it true or false? Is it beautiful or ugly? Our education ought ot help us to answer these questions.

John Masefield
Coming in solemn beauty like slow old tunes of Spain.

John Millington Synge
Every article on these islands has an almost personal character, which gives this simple life, where all art is unknown, something of the artistic beauty of medieval life.

John Milton
Beauty is nature's brag, and must be shown in courts, at feasts, and high solemnities, where most may wonder at the workmanship.

John Philip Sousa
Remember always that the composer's pen is still mightier than the bow of the violinist in you lie all the possibilities of the creation of beauty.

———

John Philip Sousa
Grand opera is the most powerful of stage appeals and that almost entirely through the beauty of music.

John Ray
Beauty is power a smile is its sword.

John Zimmerman
Beauty is often worse than wine intoxicating both the holder and beholder.

Jonathan Ive
There is beauty when something works and it works intuitively.

Jonathan Sacks
Part of the beauty of Judaism, and surely this is so for other faiths also, is that it gently restores control over time. Three times a day we stop what we are doing and turn to God in prayer. We recover perspective. We inhale a deep breath of eternity.

Jorja Fox
Beauty is everything.

Joseph Addison
A beautiful eye makes silence eloquent, a kind eye makes contradiction an assent, an enraged eye makes beauty deformed. This little member gives life to every part about us; and I believe the story of Argus implies no more, than the eye is in every part; that is to say, every other part would be mutilated, were not its force represented more by the eye than even by itself.

Joseph Brodsky
What I like about cities is that everything is king size, the beauty and the ugliness.

Josie Maran
I'm still figuring out why people would want to look at me. Maybe it's generic beauty, but it's weird to be valued for something I was born with.

Jude Law
I'm only wanted by directors for the image I give off, and it makes me angry. I always wanted to be an actor and not a beauty pageant winner.

Judith Jamison
People come to see beauty, and I dance to give it to them.

Julia Roberts
During the 80s and 90s, we all became consumed with ourselves. In the 21st century, we've come back to simpler times. People are struggling economically and this has forced them to scale back the material aspects of their lives and realise the beauty of finding the simple joy in being with the people we love.

Julie Burchill
What sort of sap doesn't know by now that picture-perfect beauty is all done with smoke and mirrors anyway?

_____

Shame, like beauty, is often in the eye of the beholder.

_____

The truth of the matter is, beauty is a specific thing, rare and fleeting. Some of us have it in our teens, 20s and 30s and then lose it most of us have it not at all. And that's perfectly okay. But lying to yourself that you have it when you don't seems to me simple-minded at best and psychotic at worst.

_____

What I find most upsetting about this new all-consuming beauty culture is that the obsession with good looks, and how you can supposedly attain them, is almost entirely female-driven.

_____

Surely being a Professional Beauty - let alone an ageing one - is one of the most insecure and doomed careers imaginable.

_____

I've always thought of beauty therapy, 'alternative' treatments and the like as the female equivalent of brothels - for essentially self-deceiving people who feel a bit hollow and have to pay to be touched.

June Jordan
There are two ways to worry words. One is hoping for the greatest possible beauty in what is created. The other is to tell the truth.

Jung Chang
I like to have Chinese furniture in my home as a constant and painful reminder of how much has been destroyed in China. The contrast between the beauty of the past and the ugliness of the modern is nowhere sharper than in China.

Junichiro Tanizaki
Find beauty not only in the thing itself but in the pattern of the shadows, the light and dark which that thing provides.

_____

We Orientals find beauty not only in the thing itself but in the pattern of the shadows, the light and darkness which that thing provides.

Justin Cronin
My theory of characterization is basically this: Put some dirt on a hero, and put some sunshine on the villain, one brush stroke of beauty on the villain.

Juvenal
Rare is the union of beauty and purity.

Karen Thompson Walker
Sometimes I think I might not have written 'The Age of Miracles' if I hadn't grown up in California, if I hadn't been exposed to its very particular blend of beauty and disaster, of danger and denial.

Katherine Hepburn
Plain women know more about men than beautiful ones do. But beautiful women don't need to know about men. It's the men who have to know about beautiful women.

Karl Wilhelm Friedrich Schlegel
Beauty is that which is simultaneously attractive and sublime.

Karolina Kurkova
The beauty comes with the balance. Everyone should find his own balance in his personal as well as his professional life. Once you do so, you will feel and look beautiful.

Kate Moss
Lila can't be a model until she's at least 21. She is already a mini-me - it is scary. She already has her own beauty kit.

Katherine Heigl
I'm really proud of myself because I've pared my beauty regimen down to a cream blush and berry-tinted lip balm, which has saved me so much time.

Kathy Ireland
Beauty comes from the inside.

Kelly Osbourne
Women are so unforgiving of themselves. We don't recognize our own beauty because we're too busy comparing ourselves to other people.

Ken Thompson
That brings me to Dennis Ritchie. Our collaboration has been a thing of beauty.

Kevin Williamson
What I loved about 'Summer' was that they were these four bright kids with a wonderful future. In a way, she was the one with the brains, and then you have the beauty queen and the jock and the introvert.

Kevyn Aucoin
Beauty has a lot to do with character.

Kevyn Aucoin
Today I see beauty everywhere I go, in every face I see, in every single soul.

Kevyn Aucoin
Soon I realized that if beauty equalled forgiveness, I was never going to be forgiven.

Khalil Gibran
Kindness is like snow. It beautifies everything it covers.

———

Of life's two chief prizes, beauty and truth, I found the first in a loving heart and the second in a laborer's hand.

———

Beauty is eternity gazing at itself in a mirror.

              ◌

Khloe Kardashian
A few years ago I lost 30 pounds, and people still wanted to criticize. And honestly, I'm happy with myself if I'm a little heavier. I realized: 'Why am I trying to conform to someone else's idea of beauty?' I think I'm beautiful either way.

Kim Alexis
A supermodel needed to be able to be on 'Sports Illustrated,' to be able to walk runways, to be able to do beauty ads, to be on covers. And the girls now can no longer be on covers and be in the ads because your actresses have taken over all the jobs. I don't know what happened, but we want our jobs back.

Kim Novak
I had a lot of resentment for a while toward Kim Novak. But I don't mind her anymore. She's okay. We've become friends. I even asked her before this trip for some beauty tips.

Kin Hubbard
Beauty is only skin deep, but it's a valuable asset if you're poor or haven't any sense.

King Hussein I
Jordan has a strange, haunting beauty and a sense of timelessness. Dotted with the ruins of empires once great, it is the last resort of yesterday in the world of tomorrow. I love every inch of it.

Kirk Gibson
I'm not out here to win a beauty contest.

Kotomichi
My heart that was rapt away by the wild cherry blossoms

Often, the roles I'm offered in England are melancholic women who are filled with regret for the past, regret for their fading beauty.
Kristin Scott Thomas

Leo Tolstoy
What a strange illusion it is to suppose that beauty is goodness.

L. Wolfe Gilbert
Those who find beauty in all of nature will find themselves at one with the secrets of life itself.

Lafcadio Hearn
But every great scripture, whether Hebrew, Indian, Persian, or Chinese, apart from its religious value will be found to have some rare and special beauty of its own and in this respect the original Bible stands very high as a monument of sublime poetry and of artistic prose.

Lara Stone
It's not like I'm sitting at home coming up with some secret beauty plan.

Lascelles Abercrombie
But the gravest difficulty, and perhaps the most important, in poetry meant solely for recitation, is the difficulty of achieving verbal beauty, or rather of making verbal beauty tell.

Lauren Conrad
I've actually spent a lot of time researching beauty products, how they are produced and how they are sold.

Lauren Graham
I didn't grow up identifying with beauty. I grew up thinking I could be smart and funny - those are the things I got feedback on.

Laurette Taylor
Personality is more important than beauty, but imagination is more important than both of them.

Laurie Holden
The beauty of 'The Walking Dead' and the beauty of being on a television show for a while, is that, it's your backstory, it's part of what you are, it's what you carry with you every day.

Lazarus Long
Delusions are often functional. A mother's opinions about her children's beauty, intelligence, goodness, et cetera ad nauseam, keep her from drowning them at birth.

Lea Michele
I am an unconventional beauty. I grew up in a high school where if you didn't have a nose job and money and if you weren't thin, you weren't cool, popular, beautiful. I was always told that I wasn't pretty enough to be on television.

Leighton Meester
I really like to be able to have variety and to try different things - that's the beauty of fashion.

Leni Riefenstahl
Through my optimism I naturally prefer and capture the beauty in life.

Leon Battista Alberti
Beauty: the adjustment of all parts proportionately so that one cannot add or subtract or change without impairing the harmony of the whole.

LeRoy Neiman
Boxing is my real passion. I can go to ballet, theatre, movies, or other sporting events... and nothing is like the fights to me. I'm excited by the visual beauty of it. A boxer can look so spectacular by doing a good job.

Leslie Jamison
Though there might not be any easy answers to the problem of poverty, its most compelling scribes do not resign themselves to representation solely for the sake of those age-old verities of truth and beauty.

Lew Wallace
Beauty is altogether in the eye of the beholder.

Lewis Carroll
Imagination is the one weapon in the war against reality.

Liam Neeson
For all of nature's wonder and beauty, it is also hostile and unpredictable.

Lillie Langtry
They saw me, those reckless seekers of beauty, and in a night I was famous.

Lily Collins
Never once does 'Snow White' herself look in the mirror so she isn't aware of her beauty or what apparently that does to people. It's really just the queen and the prince that talk about it.

Linda Evangelista
I have to hit the gym. I have beauty appointments. I have to work toward my next job and maintaining my image, just like an athlete.

Lindsay Lohan
Beauty is grace and confidence. I've learned to accept and appreciate what nature gave me.

Lindsay Wagner
Once you go inside and weed through the muck, you will find the real beauty, the truth about yourself.

Lisa Bonet
What saddens me is the corruption of youth and beauty, and the loss of soul, which is only replaced by money.

———

I have a desire to create more film, more beauty, more art, more love, but I don't feel desperate. It's not about creating or building a career.

Liv Tyler
There is no definition of beauty, but when you can see someone's spirit coming through, something unexplainable, that's beautiful to me.

———

Solitude has its own very strange beauty to it.

Lord Chesterfield
Swift speedy time, feathered with flying hours, Dissolves the beauty of the fairest brow.

Louis Kahn
Design is not making beauty, beauty emerges from selection, affinities, integration, love.

Luis Barragan
Beauty is the oracle that speaks to us all.

———

Life deprived of beauty is not worthy of being called human.

Luis Figo
I have a fantastic wife, and not only in terms of external beauty. Her priority and mine is our children. That is our choice.

Manuel Puig
I like the beauty of Faulkner's poetry. But I don't like his themes, not at all.

Marc Jacobs
I always find beauty in things that are odd and imperfect - they are much more interesting.

Marcel Duchamp
I am still a victim of chess. It has all the beauty of art - and much more. It cannot be commercialized. Chess is much purer than art in its social position.

Marcus V. Pollio
Beauty is produced by the pleasing appearance and good taste of the whole, and by the dimensions of all the parts being duly proportioned to each other.

Margaret Bourke-White
The beauty of the past belongs to the past.

Margaret Cho
I didn't appreciate the young woman that I was, or my young beauty, because I was so obsessed with the fact that I felt fat. It's never good to add to anybody else's suffering. It's an important topic to really get the gravity and the importance of - dealing with dignity.

———

Just because you are blind and unable to see my beauty doesn't mean it does not exist.

Margot Asquith
Rich men's houses are seldom beautiful, rarely comfortable, and never original. It is a constant source of surprise to people of moderate means to observe how little a big fortune contributes to Beauty.

Marguerite Gardiner
Talent, like beauty, to be pardoned, must be obscure and unostentatious.

Marguerite Young
All my writing is about the recognition that there is no single reality. But the beauty of it is that you nevertheless go on, walking towards utopia, which may not exist, on a bridge which might end before you reach the other side.

Marlene Dietrich
The average man is more interested in a woman who is interested in him than he is in a woman, any woman, with beautiful legs.

Maria Bello
I was always anti-marriage. I didn't understand monogamy. I couldn't figure out how that could last. And then I met Bryn and I started to understand the beauty of constancy and history and change and going on the roller coaster with someone - of having a partner in life.

Marie Carmichael Stopes
You can take no credit for beauty at sixteen. But if you are beautiful at sixty, it will be your own soul's doing.

Marie Stopes
You can take no credit for beauty at sixteen. But if you are beautiful at sixty, it will be your soul's own doing.

Marie von Ebner-Eschenbach
What delights us in visible beauty is the invisible.

Mariel Hemingway
I felt I had to share Idaho with my friend from New York because he'd shared New York with me, so I was going to share the beauty of nature with a man who went to museums and clubs late at night. But there was nothing to do where I lived at night.

Mario Batali
Bologna is the best city in Italy for food and has the least number of tourists. With its medieval beauty, it has it all.

Mark Burnett
I needed to be in the bush. There I find solitude and beauty and purity and focus. That's where my heart lies.

Mark Feuerstein
The closest thing I use to beauty products is the grease on the pizza from John's Pizzeria.

Marston Morse
Mathematics are the result of mysterious powers which no one understands, and which the unconscious recognition of beauty must play an important part. Out of an infinity of designs a mathematician chooses one pattern for beauty's sake and pulls it down to earth.

Martha Beck
Standards of beauty are arbitrary. Body shame exists only to the extent that our physiques don't match our own beliefs about how we should look.

———

Bracketing has turned all my experiences, remembered and present, into a gallery of miracles where I wander around dazzled by the beauty of events I cannot explain.

❧   ❧

Martina McBride
I think we should all be tolerant of each other and embrace each others' strengths and differences and uniqueness and beauty.

———

I have girls who are concerned about how they look compared to models or what have you. It's my responsibility to teach them that beauty is more than superficial.
Martina McBride

Marvin Hamlisch
Maybe I'm old-fashioned. But I remember the beauty and thrill of being moved by Broadway musicals - particularly the endings of shows.

Mary Chapin Carpenter
My sisters and I were fortunate to travel through Asia and Europe at very young ages. We confronted extraordinary beauty in Athens and unspeakable poverty in India.

Mary MacLane
I do not see any beauty in self-restraint.

Mary McDonnell
We have to get back to the beauty of just being alive in this present moment.

Mary-Louise Parker
My mother is a beauty.

Mason
Time's gradual touch has moulder'd into beauty many a tower which when it frown'd with all its battlements, was only terrible.

Matthew Arnold
Poetry a criticism of life under the conditions fixed for such a criticism by the laws of poetic truth and poetic beauty.

Matthew Fox
If you look closely at a tree you'll notice it's knots and dead branches, just like our bodies. What we learn is that beauty and imperfection go together wonderfully.

———

Beauty saves. Beauty heals. Beauty motivates. Beauty unites. Beauty returns us to our origins, and here lies the ultimate act of saving, of healing, of overcoming dualism.

———

Do not confuse beauty with beautiful. Beautiful is a human judgment. Beauty is All. The difference is everything.

Matthew Prior
For, when with beauty we can virtue join, we paint the semblance of a form divine.

Max Bill
Far from creating a new formalism, what these can yield is something far transcending surface values since they not only embody form as beauty, but also form in which intuitions or ideas or conjectures have taken visible substance.

Max Roach
Jazz is a very democratic musical form. It comes out of a communal experience. We take our respective instruments and collectively create a thing of beauty.

Maya Angelou
We delight in the beauty of the butterfly, but rarely admit the changes it has gone through to achieve that beauty.

Meagan Good
The beauty of having short hair is that I actually can wash and style it at home!

Meryl Streep
I didn't have any confidence in my beauty when I was young. I felt like a character actress, and I still do.

Michael Franti
All the freaky people make the beauty of the world.

Michael K. Powell
So as I look at transitioning to the communication platforms of the future, I see that the beauty of Internet protocols is you get the separation of the layers between service and technology.

Michael Stipe
So, we just kind of created our own thing and that's part of the beauty of Athens: is that it's so off the map and there's no way you could ever be the East Village or an L.A. scene or a San Francisco scene, that it just became its own thing.

Michel Gondry
The beauty of doing film is that you construct whatever you do block by block and you can build something that will stay.

Mike Figgis
There's a sadness to the human condition that I think music is good for. It gives a counterpoint to the visual beauty, and adds depth to pictures that they wouldn't have if the music wasn't there.

Mike Judge
Beauty and the Beast seemed like it all was really brown. The whole thing was just so brown and orange and yellow, like Burger King or something. I don't think I would have liked Beauty and the Beast at any age.

Mike Weir
The beauty of golf, you're in charge out here.

Minna Antrim
The very women who object to the morals of a notoriously beautiful actress, grow big with pride when an admirer suggests their marked resemblance to this stage beauty in physique.

Miranda Kerr
I live by the philosophy that beauty starts from within, and I make a conscious effort to fill my body with nutrients through the food I eat.

———

Everyone has a different beauty and different qualities and I think that women need to learn to love their qualities and be comfortable in the fact that everyone is different.

Mireille Enos
I know as an actor there is a certain liberation auditioning for a role that has no beauty requirements.

Miriam Beard
One must learn, if one is to see the beauty in Japan, to like an extraordinarily restrained and delicate loveliness.

Miuccia Prada
Fashion fosters cliches of beauty, but I want to tear them apart.

———

I always loved aesthetics. Not particularly fashion, but an idea of beauty.

———

Now, I'm not saying I'm fashionable, but there are sociological interests that matter to me, things that are theoretical, political, intellectual and also concerned with vanity and beauty that we all think about but that I try to mix up and translate into fashion.

Mos Def
With guys I revere, like Marcus Garvey or Malcolm X, their look is less about style than purpose and the expression of beauty. It wasn't just about being noticed, you know?

Moses Mendelssohn
Instead, it appears to be a particular mark of beauty that it is considered with tranquil satisfaction that it pleases if we also do not possess it and we are still far removed from demanding to possess it.

Mstislav Rostropovich
People are craving this great progress in electronics, going after computers, the Internet, etc. It's a giant progress technologically. But they must have a balance of soul, a balance for human beauty. That means art has an important role.

Mstislav Rostropovich
Baalbek is so beautiful. It is the heart of beauty in the Middle East - I want to embrace these people with my music. I will try so hard for them. Their president is a Christian, their prime minister is a Muslim. Music is for everyone.

Munshi Premchand
Beauty doesn't need ornaments. Softness can't bear the weight of ornaments.

Murray Kempton
The beauty of a strong, lasting commitment is often best understood by men incapable of it.

Nadine Gordimer
Truth isn't always beauty, but the hunger for it is.

Naomi Wolf
No matter what a woman's appearance may be, it will be used to undermine what she is saying and taken to individualize - as her personal problem - observations she makes about the beauty myth in society.

Narada Michael Walden
I'm very proud of my love for Whitney Houston. She really changed my life. She made my life a better life. She was so beautiful in her love for God, her love for her family and her love for music. She truly loved her music. She could do everything! She had flawless rhythm, flawless pitch, flawless feeling, and flawless beauty.

—

I first fell in love with music when I was a little boy. When I first heard music, I felt the beauty in it. Then, being able to tap along on a table top and box was great, but my favorite thing to do was to watch records spin. I would almost get hypnotized by it. These things are what drew me in initially.

Natalia Vodianova
When you are at the bottom, you find beauty in such little things, and goodness in such little gestures. When I compare any struggle today to ones that I may have had in my childhood, there is nothing that can bring me down.

Natasha Henstridge
My main aim has always been to do good quality films with roles that have some substance. With Power and Beauty there were loads of things that I liked about the movie, which made me opt for it.

Naya Rivera
I will admit to hoarding beauty products. I'm a beauty lady.

Neil Gaiman
Because, if one is writing novels today, concentrating on the beauty of the prose is right up there with concentrating on your semi-colons, for wasted effort.

Nigel Barker
I have a book out called 'The Beauty Equation' and it discusses how off track we have gone in considering beauty.

Nikolai Gogol
Always think of what is useful and not what is beautiful. Beauty will come of its own accord.

Nikos Kazantzakis
Beauty is merciless. You do not look at it, it looks at you and does not forgive.

Nina Dobrev
I was kind of a jock in school. Beauty wasn't something I spent a lot of time on.

Ninon de L'Enclos
The ideal has many names, and beauty is but one of them.

Octavia Spencer
I hope that in some way that I can be some sort of beacon of hope, especially because I am not the typical Hollywood beauty.

Oliver Goldsmith
Romance and novel paint beauty in colors more charming than nature, and describe a happiness that humans never taste. How deceptive and destructive are those pictures of consummate bliss!

Oliver Wendell Holmes
Wisdom is the abstract of the past, but beauty is the promise of the future.

Olivia Colman
I feel fortunate that I'm not a beauty. I'm not a classic beauty. I feel it is harder for girls who are like that. There are fewer parts.

Ossie Davis
I find, in being black, a thing of beauty: a joy a strength a secret cup of gladness.

Ouida
Familiarity is a magician that is cruel to beauty but kind to ugliness.

Ovid
Beauty is a fragile gift.

Pam Grier
I grew up in a family where we weren't allowed to talk about beauty or to put any emphasis on physical appearance.

———

This whole beauty thing is something I've never comprehended.

Pamela Anderson
Natural beauty takes at least two hours in front of a mirror.

———

I was never an ambitious girl, or even a self-confident one. I never went in for beauty pageants or wore a stitch of make-up until I went to Los Angeles.

Pat Metheny
The beauty of jazz is that it's malleable. People are addressing it to suit their own personalities.

Patricia Sun
We have magnificent brains, but we use a great deal of our brilliance to keep ourselves stuck and ignorant, to keep ourselves from not shining. We are so afraid of our beauty and radiance and brilliance because it scared the adults around us when we were children.

Paul Gauguin
Art requires philosophy, just as philosophy requires art. Otherwise, what would become of beauty?

Paul Getty
The beauty one can find in art is one of the pitifully few real and lasting products of human endeavor.

Paul Klee
Beauty is as relative as light and dark. Thus, there exists no beautiful woman, none at all, because you are never certain that a still far more beautiful woman will not appear and completely shame the supposed beauty of the first.

Paulina Porizkova
Beauty, unlike the rest of the gifts handed out at birth, does not require dedication, patience and hard work to pay off. But it's also the only gift that does not keep on giving.

Paz Vega
Asian people have a unique way about them and a different sense of beauty. It's exotic to me. I like they way Asians project their feelings. There's a hardness to the culture, but at the same time there's a delicateness.

Pearl S. Buck
Order is the shape upon which beauty depends.

Peggy Fleming
I think exercise tests us in so many ways, our skills, our hearts, our ability to bounce back after setbacks. This is the inner beauty of sports and competition, and it can serve us all well as adult athletes.

Percy Bysshe Shelley
Poetry lifts the veil from the hidden beauty of the world, and makes familiar objects be as if they were not familiar.

———

Obscenity, which is ever blasphemy against the divine beauty in life, is a monster for which the corruption of society forever brings forth new food, which it devours in secret.

Peter Latham
Perfect health, like perfect beauty, is a rare thing and so, it seems, is perfect disease.

Peter Nivio Zarlenga
Beauty is being in harmony with what you are.

Peter York
If beauty isn't genius it usually signals at least a high level of animal cunning.

Petrarch
Rarely do great beauty and great virtue dwell together.

Phil Ochs
In such ugly times, the only true protest is beauty.

Philip Roth
Literature isn't a moral beauty contest. Its power arises from the authority and audacity with which the impersonation is pulled off the belief it inspires is what counts.

One night I'll be in Los Angeles and it'll be a Latin crowd, and then another night I'll go to Fresno and it'll be an all-black crowd. To me, that's the beauty of the music.
Pitbull

I would rather be adorned by beauty of character than jewels. Jewels are the gift of fortune, while character comes from within.
Plautus

Pope Paul VI
Liturgy is like a strong tree whose beauty is derived from the continuous renewal of its leaves, but whose strength comes from the old trunk, with solid roots in the ground.

Rabindranath Tagore
Beauty is truth's smile when she beholds her own face in a perfect mirror.

Rachel Bilson
My quick beauty tip is always have a tinted gloss of some kind to give you some color even if you have no makeup on.

_____

I think beauty comes from within, and society paints a ridiculous picture.

_____

My daily beauty regimen consists of washing my face before bed and putting on moisturizer.

_____

My unusual beauty tip is that I often use Vaseline to take my make up off. It works great and is good for sensitive skin.

Rachel Bilson
I envy the sensibility in Europe, appreciating beauty in women as they age. I'm going to go that way. I might dye my gray hair for a bit, but beyond that the buck stops. I'm not having any work done.

Rachel McAdams
My mother never put an emphasis on looks. She let us grow up on our own time line. She never forced any beauty regimen into my world.

Rachel Roy
I have a real passion for many aspects of home lifestyle and beauty.

Rachel Stevens
I know it sounds a bit corny, but I do think that beauty and sexiness come from within.

Rachel Weisz
As Ralph's character begins to discover the political thriller aspect of the film, he falls deeper in love with his wife, so the two run together. That's the beauty of this film. It has fast pace and excitement, but it also has heart and soul.

Ralph Venning
All the beauty of the world, 'tis but skin deep.

Ralph Waldo Emerson
To laugh often and love much; to win the respect of intelligent persons and the affection of children; to earn the approbation of honest citizens and endure the betrayal of false friends; to appreciate beauty; to find the best in others; to give of one's self; to leave the world a bit better, whether by a healthy child, a garden patch or a redeemed social condition; to have played and laughed with enthusiasm and sung with exultation; to know even one life has breathed easier because you have lived - this is to have succeeded.

———

Beauty without grace is the hook without the bait.

———

A beautiful form is better than a beautiful face; it gives a higher pleasure than statues or pictures; it is the finest of the fine arts.

———

Love of beauty is taste. The creation of beauty is art.

———

Flowers... are a proud assertion that a ray of beauty outvalues all the utilities of the world.

Rashida Jones
Smiling is definitely one of the best beauty remedies. If you have a good sense of humor and a good approach to life, that's beautiful.

———

I pretty much borrow my entire beauty regime from my mom.

———

Ads featuring real women and real beauty are such a necessary component to offset the potentially dangerous programming out there for little girls.

Rem Koolhaas
We say we want to create beauty, identity, quality, singularity. And yet, maybe in truth these cities that we have are desired. Maybe their very characterlessness provides the best context for living.

Renee Vivien
I have no right to beauty. I had been condemned to masculine ugliness.

Richard Armour
Beauty is only skin deep, and the world is full of thin skinned people.

Richard Cecil
Every year of my life I grow more convinced that it is wisest and best to fix our attention on the beautiful and the good, and dwell as little as possible on the evil and the false.

Richard H. Baker
For most people, we often marvel at the beauty of a sunrise or the magnificence of a full moon, but it is impossible to fathom the magnitude of the universe that surrounds us.

Richard Le Gallienne
It is curious how, from time immemorial, man seems to have associated the idea of evil with beauty, shrunk from it with a sort of ghostly fear, while, at the same time drawn to it by force of its hypnotic attraction.

———

The beauty we love is very silent. It smiles softly to itself, but never speaks.

———

We also maintain - again with perfect truth - that mystery is more than half of beauty, the element of strangeness that stirs the senses through the imagination.

Richard Steele
To give pain is the tyranny; to make happy, the true empire of beauty.

———

Nothing can atone for the lack of modesty without which beauty is ungraceful and wit detestable.

Rima Fakih
I'm not a party animal I took my job as Miss USA very seriously... Sometimes, of course, I want to let it all go. Even though I'm a beauty queen, you're also an unofficial ambassador, and there's a lot of pressure.

Robert Bridges
Beauty, the eternal Spouse of the Wisdom of God and Angel of his Presence thru' all creation.

Robert Browning
I trust in nature for the stable laws of beauty and utility. Spring shall plant and autumn garner to the end of time.

Robert Caro
I really wanted there to be something in my life that I enjoy just for the beauty of it.

———

The New York City Ballet is obviously speaking to a whole new generation and bringing it the same wonder and beauty that it brought previous generations.

Robert Mapplethorpe
Beauty and the devil are the same thing.

———

I am obsessed with beauty. I want everything to be perfect, and of course it isn't. And that's a tough place to be because you're never satisfied.

Robert Motherwell
Walk on a rainbow trail walk on a trail of song, and all about you will be beauty. There is a way out of every dark mist, over a rainbow trail.

Robert Musil
The thought came to me that all one loves in art becomes beautiful. Beauty is nothing but the expression of the fact that something is being loved. Only thus could she be defined.

Robert Plant
It's not some great work of beauty and love to be a rock-and-roll singer.

Roberto Benigni
My duty is to try to reach beauty. Cinema is emotion. When you laugh you cry.

Roberto Cavalli
I really admire a woman for her intelligence, her personality. Beauty is not enough.

Robin Roberts
My mama told me in college, 'I love you, and you're God's child, but natural beauty will only take you so far.'

Robin Wright Penn
It's just poetry, beauty and love. How hard can that be to act?

Sir Roger Penrose
But I think it is a serious issue to wonder about the other platonic absolutes of say beauty and morality.

Ron Ben-Israel
Pastry is different from cooking because you have to consider the chemistry, beauty and flavor. It's not just sugar and eggs thrown together. I tell my pastry chefs to be in tune for all of this. You have to be challenged by using secret or unusual ingredients.

Rosalind Russell
Where is there beauty when you see deprivation and starvation?

Rosanna Arquette
It's not fair the emphasis put on beauty, or on sexuality.

Rose Schneiderman
Surely these women won't lose any more of their beauty and charm by putting a ballot in a ballot box once a year than they are likely to lose standing in foundries or laundries all year round. There is no harder contest than the contest for bread, let me tell you that.

Rowan D. Williams
So every creative act strives to attain an absolute status it longs to create a world of beauty to triumph over chaos and convert it to order.

Roy Ayers
The true beauty of music is that it connects people. It carries a message, and we, the musicians, are the messengers.

Roy Barnes
We live in a state with a wonderful climate and plenty of natural beauty, from the shores of Cumberland Island to the Chattahoochee River to the Blue Ridge Mountains.

Rudolf Otto
A child does not notice the greatness and the beauty of nature and the splendor of God in his works.

I've developed into quite a swan. I'm one of those people that will probably look better and better as I get older until I drop dead of beauty.
Rufus Wainwright

Ruth St. Denis
The real message of the Dance opens up the vistas of life to all who have the urge to express beauty with no other instrument than their own bodies, with no apparatus and no dependence on anything other than space.

Saint Augustine
Since love grows within you, so beauty grows. For love is the beauty of the soul.

_____

Beauty is indeed a good gift of God but that the good may not think it a great good, God dispenses it even to the wicked.

People often say that 'beauty is in the eye of the beholder,' and I say that the most liberating thing about beauty is realizing that you are the beholder. This empowers us to find beauty in places where others have not dared to look, including inside ourselves.
Salma Hayek

Samuel Daniel
Beauty, sweet love, is like the morning dew, Whose short refresh upon tender green, Cheers for a time, but till the sun doth show And straight is gone, as it had never been.

Sara Teasdale
Beauty, more than bitterness, makes the heart break.

_____

Oh who can tell the range of joy or set the bounds of beauty?

Sarah Bernhardt
What matters poverty? What matters anything to him who is enamoured of our art? Does he not carry in himself every joy and every beauty?

———

The truth, the absolute truth, is that the chief beauty for the theatre consists in fine bodily proportions.

෴

Saskya Pandita
Even in decline, a virtuous man increases the beauty of his behavior. A burning stick, though turned to the ground, has its flame drawn upwards.

Scott Weiland
There's a beauty in being part of a band, when there's equality and trust.

———

Music, as many people have said, is the universal language. Of course points are made which make you think about things, but ultimately it makes you feel. And that's why people remember more songs that have meant something during their life than films. They start to define periods in your life, and that's kind of the beauty of it.

෴

Selma Blair
I used to wear a lot of red lipstick, and when I got a pimple, I'd cover it up with eyeliner to turn it into a beauty mark.

———

I'm flatchested, I'm short, I'm brunette, I have droopy eyes, and so people have a hard time casting me as a 'beauty.'

෴

Serge Gainsbourg
Ugliness is in a way superior to beauty because it lasts.

———

It is important to fund young researchers who want to do curiosity-driven research. Curiosity-driven research is a part of life. Some people are curious. They want to learn more about nature and society should help that. It's like art: you can learn more and bring more beauty.

Sharon Stone
I thought it might be a good move to get into a beauty contest so I tried for Miss Pennsylvania and won. I think that helped me get noticed, at least by the people of Pennsylvania.

Sharon Tate
My definition of love is being full. Complete. It makes everything lighter. Beauty is something you see. Love is something you feel.

Shay Mitchell
My daily beauty regimen is definitely always in the mornings, and at night, always washing my face with a basic cleanser. I also use a moisturizer with SPF to follow up.

Shay Mitchell
We all have to find beauty within us, as opposed to just our exterior.

Sherri Shepherd
Wigs have always been a part of my life and have become a staple accessory in my closet. I can remember being a little girl and hearing all the commotion in my house from my mom, aunts and grandmother when picking out their wigs for the day. It was such a good time for them and part of their everyday beauty routine.

Sheryl Crow
The beauty of having a producer is that you have someone who says, You're finished.

Shirley MacLaine
I wasn't afraid of getting old, because I was never a great beauty.

————

I mean, no one asks beauty secrets of me, or 'What size do you wear?' or 'Who's your couturier?' They ask me about really deep things and I love that.

Shirley Manson
People don't associate red hair, pale skin, and freckles with beauty.

Sloane Crosley
You can't possibly fathom the ins and outs of a prepubescent beauty treatment until you've felt the strange but exhilarating tingle of a cottage-cheese-and-Pop-Rocks facial.

Socrates
No man has the right to be an amateur in the matter of physical training. It is a shame for a man to grow old without seeing the beauty and strength of which his body is capable.

Beauty is a short-lived tyranny.

Sophia Loren
Nothing makes a woman more beautiful than the belief she is beautiful.

Sophie Thompson
I've just finished reading a book about the brilliant Margaret Rutherford. She wasn't a beauty, but inside she was absolutely blazing and passionate about her work. She's one of those life-affirming characters.

St. Jerome
Beauty when unadorned is adorned the most.

Stephen Collins
Part of the beauty of the show in a way is that he's not perfect, but you can always count on him to do the right thing in a pinch. That's why he inspires people and inspires me.

Stephen Fry
I've never had any illusions about being a lead actor in films, because lead actors have to be of a certain kind. Apart from the beauty of looks and figure, which I cannot claim to have, there's just a particular kind of ordinary-Joe quality that a film star needs to have.

Story Musgrave
It's hard to say what drives a three year-old, but I think I had a sense that nature was my solace, and nature was a place in which there was beauty, in which there was order.

Studs Terkel
I want, of course, peace, grace, and beauty. How do you do that? You work for it.

Susan Estrich
I'm always suspicious of really beautiful women telling us we shouldn't be worried about beauty.

Susan Sontag
The past itself, as historical change continues to accelerate, has become the most surreal of subjects - making it possible... to see a new beauty in what is vanishing.

Susie Orbach
Beauty has been democratised. No longer the preserve of movie stars and models but available to all. But while the invitation to beauty is welcomed, it has become not so much an option as an imperative.

Sydney J. Harris
The beauty of 'spacing' children many years apart lies in the fact that parents have time to learn the mistakes that were made with the older ones - which permits them to make exactly the opposite mistakes with the younger ones.

Sydney Smith
Do not try to push your way through to the front ranks of your profession do not run after distinctions and rewards but do your utmost to find an entry into the world of beauty.

Sylvia Kristel
I have a talent for happiness. I look with the eyes of a painter, and I see beauty.

Tadao Ando
There is a role and function for beauty in our time.

_____

People tend not to use this word beauty because it's not intellectual - but there has to be an overlap between beauty and intellect.

Tahar Ben Jelloun
Beauty is first and foremost an emotion.

Teri Hatcher
In all my career, in my ups and downs, I've never had a beauty campaign. This was meaningful that at almost 41 years old, I could be getting my first beauty campaign. It made me feel really great.

_____

I'm 40 and I just got my first beauty campaign with Clairol Nice and Easy.

_____

This was meaningful that at almost 41 years old, I could be getting my first beauty campaign.

145

Theodore Bikel
I tried for a while to be an agricultural worker and was hopelessly bored. To me it was meaningless. I would stand around in heaps of manure and sings about the beauty of the work I wasn't doing.

_____

I tried for a while to be an agricultural worker and was hopelessly bored. I would stand around in heaps of manure and sing about the beauty of the work I wasn't doing.

Art is beauty, the perpetual invention of detail, the choice of words, the exquisite care of execution.
Theophile Gautier

Thomas Campbell
Beauty's tears are lovelier than her smile.

Thomas Kincade
Everyone can identify with a fragrant garden, with beauty of sunset, with the quiet of nature, with a warm and cozy cottage.

_____

People who put my paintings on their walls are putting their values on their walls: faith, family, home, a simpler way of living, the beauty of nature, quiet, tranquillity, peace, joy, hope. They beckon you into this world that provides an alternative to your nightly news broadcast.

Thomas Mann
For I must tell you that we artists cannot tread the path of Beauty without Eros keeping company with us and appointing himself as our guide.

_____

Solitude gives birth to the original in us, to beauty unfamiliar and perilous - to poetry. But also, it gives birth to the opposite: to the perverse, the illicit, the absurd.

Thomas Nash
Beauty is but a flower, which wrinkles will devour.

Thornton Wilder
It is very necessary to have markers of beauty left in a world seemingly bent on making the most evil ugliness.

Tia Carrere

Doors open because you're beautiful, but I wouldn't cultivate beauty to the exclusion of brains.

––––

Beauty lasts five minutes. Maybe longer if you have a good plastic surgeon.

Tia Mowry

I like to embrace natural beauty. I try to get at least 8 hours of sleep, drinking a lot of water and exercising.

Tila Tequila

This is so cliche, but my beauty icon would have to be Angelina Jolie. She looks like she wears natural makeup, but she's still beautiful.

––––

I think every person has their own identity and beauty. Everyone being different is what is really beautiful. If we were all the same, it would be boring.

Tim Vine

Black beauty - he's a dark horse.

Tobey Maguire

I might have some character traits that some might see as innocence or naive. That's because I discovered peace and happiness in my soul. And with this knowledge, I also see the beauty of human life.

Tom Ford

I think the 1970s will always be the decade for me. Obviously, I grew up in that era, but the beauty standard was touchable, kissable.

Tom Perrotta

I read 'The Great Gatsby' in high school and was hypnotized by the beauty of the sentences and moved by the story about the irrevocability of lost love.

Tom Udall

The sport of horse racing which, at its best, showcases the majestic beauty of this animal and the athleticism of jockeys, has reached an alarming level of corruption and exploitation.

Tom Wolfe
This is the artist, then, life's hungry man, the glutton of eternity, beauty's miser, glory's slave.

Tony Kushner
Who knows better than artists how much ugliness there is on the way to beauty, how many ghastly, mortifying missteps, how many days of granitic blockheadedness and dismaying ineptitude there is on the way to accomplishment, how partial all accomplishment is, how incomplete?

Valentino Garavani
I love my beauty. It's not my fault.

Van Morrison
Every performance is different. That's the beauty of it.

Vera Brittain
There is an abiding beauty which may be appreciated by those who will see things as they are and who will ask for no reward except to see.

Vera Farmiga
Editing yourself is like an irksome coin toss. You've got to strip yourself of super ego and operate from the id. Maybe I've got my Freud mixed up. It's just hard to trade a beauty shot for the performance with truth and a brightly lit zit.

Vernon Howard
Beauty is only skin deep, but it's a valuable asset if you're poor or haven't any sense.

Victor Hugo
To love beauty is to see light.

———

Dear God! how beauty varies in nature and art. In a woman the flesh must be like marble in a statue the marble must be like flesh.

Victoria Justice
It's nice to just embrace the natural beauty within you.

Victoria Legrand
I like to find the beauty in the ugly. When I'm in a thrift store, I gravitate toward pieces I know I'll wear a ton, and insane pieces that I'm sure most people would consider gross. But I find them inspiring. Our van is currently stocked with some of my random findings from this tour. Maybe I'll call my aesthetic 'van fashion.'

Vince Gill
The real beauty of it - key to my life was playing key chords on a banjo. For somebody else it may be a golf club that mom and dad put in their hands or a baseball or ballet lessons. Real gift to give to me and put it in writing.

Vincent Cassel
I have learned that acting is not about beauty.

Virginia Woolf
The beauty of the world has two edges, one of laughter, one of anguish, cutting the heart asunder.

Vivien Leigh
People think that if you look fairly reasonable, you can't possibly act, and as I only care about acting, I think beauty can be a great handicap.

Vivienne Westwood
My beauty secret is absolutely no sun.

Vladimir Kramnik
For me art and chess are closely related, both are forms in which the self finds beauty and expression.

_____

I believe every chess player senses beauty, when he succeeds in creating situations, which contradict the expectations and the rules, and he succeeds in mastering this situation.

_____

The development of beauty in chess never depends on you alone. No matter how much imagination and creativity you invest, you still do not create beauty. Your opponent must react at the same highest level.

_____

Even if you play perfectly, a fault of your opponent's can destroy the entire beauty of the game.

_____

When I speak of the beauty of a game of chess, then naturally this is subjective. Beauty can be found in a very technical, mathematical game for example. That is the beauty of clarity.

Walter Raleigh
Remember if you marry for beauty, thou bindest thyself all thy life for that which perchance, will neither last nor please thee one year: and when thou hast it, it will be to thee of no price at all.

149

W. H. Davies
As long as I love Beauty I am young.

Wallace Stevens
Death is the mother of Beauty hence from her, alone, shall come fulfillment to our dreams and our desires.

———

I do not know which to prefer, The beauty of inflections, Or the beauty of innuendoes, The blackbird whistling, Or just after.

Walter Benjamin
The idea that happiness could have a share in beauty would be too much of a good thing.

Walter Pater
Many attempts have been made by writers on art and poetry to define beauty in the abstract, to express it in the most general terms, to find some universal formula for it.

———

Such discussions help us very little to enjoy what has been well done in art or poetry, to discriminate between what is more and what is less excellent in them, or to use words like beauty, excellence, art, poetry, with a more precise meaning than they would otherwise have.

———

What is important, then, is not that the critic should possess a correct abstract definition of beauty for the intellect, but a certain kind of temperament, the power of being deeply moved by the presence of beautiful objects.

———

One of the most beautiful passages of Rousseau is that in the sixth book of Confessions, where he describes the awakening in him of the literary sense. Of such wisdom, the poetic passion, the desire of beauty, the love of art for its own sake, has most.

William Arthur Ward
A warm smile is the universal language of kindness.

William Allen Butler
And queenly is the state she keeps, In beauty's lofty trust secure.

William C. Bryant
A sculptor wields The chisel, and the stricken marble grows To beauty.

William Shakespeare
To thine own self be true, and it must follow, as the night the day, thou canst not then be false to any man.

William S. Burrows
What does the money machine eat? It eats youth, spontaneity, life, beauty, and, above all, it eats creativity. It eats quality and shits quantity.

William Shenstone
Grandeur and beauty are so very opposite, that you often diminish the one as you increase the other. Variety is most akin to the latter, simplicity to the former.

William Temple
You may keep your beauty and your health, unless you destroy them yourself, or discourage them to stay with you, by using them ill.

Xenophon
For what the horse does under compulsion, as Simon also observes, is done without understanding and there is no beauty in it either, any more than if one should whip and spur a dancer.

———

A horse is a thing of beauty... none will tire of looking at him as long as he displays himself in his splendor.

Yusef Lateef
When the soul looks out of its body, it should see only beauty in its path. These are the sights we must hold in mind, in order to move to a higher place.

Zac Posen
I don't believe in one ideal beauty.

Zachary Levi
Being nerdy just means being passionate about something, including everyone - the coolest people on Earth are passionate and therefore nerdy about something whatever it is, whether it's sports, or gaming, or technology, or fashion, or beauty, or food, or whatever.

Zoe Saldana

I'm very accepting with my age. It's like notches on your belt: experience, wisdom, and a different kind of beauty. There comes a day when you've become comfortable in your skin.

I hope you have enjoyed this.

If you have,
please leave me a review on Amazon.

And check out some more in the series
(more being added all the time!)

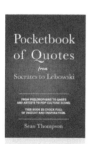   

Made in United States
Cleveland, OH
09 December 2024

11603923R00089